PRAISE FOR CRAZY

"Lyn has written a truly healing memoir, not just in terms of its focus on emotional wholeness, but as an invitation to bring healing to your life. This text is about integrity of spirit, of becoming a whole person, and not just dissociative identity disorder. As I read the book, I reflected on my own experiences of conflict and trauma, their impact on my personal and professional life, and my own quest for spiritual integrity, bringing together the many facets of my experience from childhood to retirement in a dynamic tapestry of wholeness. Personal and provocative, Lyn's memoir will invite you to embark on a holy adventure of self-awareness, healing, and spiritual transformation. I highly recommend this book to anyone seeking greater self-knowledge and awareness of the struggles everyone faces. To read it is to awaken to the healing resources Lyn experiences and the healing resources you can experience in your own journey toward wholeness and integrity. I am grateful for Lyn's courageous and life-transforming witness."

—REV. DR. BRUCE EPPERLY, Process Theologian, Author of *Healing Marks: Healing and Spirituality in Mark's Gospel*

"*Crazy* is a wonderful example of overcoming adversity and reclaiming your life with fragmented traumatic memory. Lyn shares the honest and hard journey of recovering from a difficult childhood through hard therapeutic work and honoring her growing faith."

—JAIME POLLOCK, Founder and Director of An Infinite Mind

"*Crazy* is a beautifully written, exceptionally honest story of hope and recovery, and a beacon of hope to those who still suffer from the effects of childhood sexual abuse and emotional wounding."

—REV. TILDA NORBERG, Mdiv, Founder of Gestalt Pastoral Care, Author of *Consenting to Grace: An Introduction to Gestalt Pastoral Care*

"Much has been researched and written about DID, largely by professionals. It is an act of courage for someone with DID to describe the grueling search for a modicum of normality: a life free of inner conflict and the celebration of the present. Lyn Barrett's memoir describes that journey, the gift of a full life, with a rich description of both."

—SONIA NOWAK, LCSW

"Lyn's compelling personal journey to uncovering her traumatic past pulls the reader in from the first page. Her descent into the internal chaos of dissociative identity disorder provides a window into the profound impact of childhood trauma, and the exquisite way the brain copes. Lyn's lyrical prose carefully weaves a poignant story about the exceptional courage and strength it takes to heal from severe trauma. This book is essential reading for any mental health professional working with a client diagnosed with a dissociative disorder."

—FRANCES A. KELLEY, Ph.D., Professor of Psychology, Carlow University

"Lyn highlights what most who live outside of the world of dissociation would perceive as 'crazy,' but that I would challenge as creative, adaptive, and nuanced. With her courage to share the details of her life and the unfolding and identifying of her system, she reveals the depth of work that is done to find cooperation, consensus, and unity where it can be found. Sometimes troubling, sometimes ingratiating . . . as we who share this experience know, our alters come into existence for our survival and then for our peace. I write here with gratitude, as DID is becoming demystified to the ordinary public and embraced by the extraordinary."

—JANE TAMBREE, LCSW-C, Psychiatric and Forensic Clinician

"*Crazy: Reclaiming Life from the Shadow of Traumatic Memory* is a precious, deeply honest, and moving healing journey through the ups and downs of living with dissociative identity disorder. I believe one of Lyn's greatest contributions in courageously sharing her story is the hope that springs forth from its pages. Those who have experienced the trauma of abuse and those who find themselves wandering through the complicated world of alters would benefit by reading Lyn's story. As one who often ministers with adults who were abused as children, I would put *Crazy* top on my list of valuable resources in support of their healing process. I would highly recommend that those who are helpers in the process read this powerful memoir, too. As Lyn's friend exclaimed in her memoir, 'We're not just survivors, we're thrivers!' and that means others can become 'thrivers,' too!"

—REV. WANDA D. CRANER, President of Gestalt Pastoral Care Associates, Inc.

"Barrett's prose style is precise and rich, and she excels at communicating her complex emotional states, keeping the reader grounded even when she describes the experience of switching between personalities. . . . A compelling exploration of a misunderstood disorder and of the various ways it can complicate a person's life. An engaging and deeply felt account of mental illness."

—KIRKUS REVIEW

Crazy: Reclaiming Life from the Shadow of Traumatic Memory

by Lyn Barrett

ISBN 978-1-64663-543-6

Published by

köehlerbooks™

3705 Shore Drive
Virginia Beach, VA 23455
800-435-4811
www.koehlerbooks.com

ber 2021
Kim,
May we — together —
we wide publicity to
this badly needed mental
health memoir. Here's to the
journey! *Lyn Barrett*

CRAZY

*Reclaiming Life from the
Shadow of Traumatic Memory*

LYN BARRETT

VIRGINIA BEACH
CAPE CHARLES

Dedicated to Sonia,
who helped me give birth to myself . . .

. . . and to the community of courageous women and men with DID
who are not crazy but have used a brilliant coping strategy
to survive the crazy things that were done to them.

AUTHOR'S NOTE

Passages in italics are either taken directly from my journals or denote technical words followed by definitions. Italicized passages in quotation marks were spoken aloud by my alters.

To protect the privacy of my adult children, the children in this memoir have been fictionalized. In some cases, other names and identifying characteristics have been changed to protect the privacy of the people depicted.

Cognitive memory is fluid; this story is true to the best of my cognitive memory. Traumatic memory is frozen and more reliable than cognitive memory. Therefore, passages relating traumatic memory are reliable, although sometimes confusing.

"Hope is the thing with feathers that perches in the soul and sings the tune without the words and never stops at all."

EMILY DICKENSON

"Never, never, never give up."

WINSTON CHURCHILL

TABLE OF CONTENTS

FOREWORD

In her unforgettable memoir, Lyn Barrett helps us grasp how childhood trauma can be deeply hidden from our consciousness, and that the deeper truth of what happened can be discovered and healed even when cognitive memory remains elusive.

A detailed narrative memory is the prized standard for truth in our culture. Yet we know, through the work of Dr. Bessel van der Kolk and other pioneers in the field of trauma, that *The Body Keeps the Score* (Penguin Books, 2015) and that traumatic memories often do not reside in our cognitive brain but in dissociated fragments that seem to burst into our awareness out of nowhere. In a survivor with dissociative identity disorder (DID), some of those fragments take on distinct personalities and roles, all created with a very specific and protective purpose.

In her memoir, Lyn takes us inside her internal alter system developed to protect her from the unbearable weight of full knowledge of what was happening to her as a child. Her story is a gift for all the survivors of childhood sexual abuse whose chronically hurting bodies, fractured relationships, depression, anxiety, eating disorders, suicidal ideation, self-harming behavior, and so much more are evidence of crimes committed against them for which only whisps of cognitive memory can be found.

Courts can convict a person of murder without a body, given a strong presentation of evidence that renders a verdict beyond a reasonable doubt by twelve peers. Yet those sexually abused as children often interrogate themselves mercilessly, demanding details of who, what, how, where, when, searching desperately for clear, compelling memory of what exactly happened. Echoes of childhood violence whisper from the shadows, press for release from the hidden chambers of the mind, and ripple through the body as pain.

I got to know Lyn when she was studying at Lancaster Theological Seminary in Pennsylvania. I occasionally taught classes on religious response to child sexual abuse at the seminary at the invitation of Dr. Frank Stalfa, a scholar and pastoral counselor who encouraged me to weave my own experience of severe childhood trauma into the liberation theology that captivated me during my work with displaced people in El Salvador during the years of bloody civil war.

At the time, I was directing programs on family-violence prevention at a counseling center, and my book *The Deepest Wound: How a Journey to El Salvador Led to Healing from Mother-Daughter Incest* (Writer's Showcase, 2001) had been recently published, which Lyn discovered when she was browsing through the seminary's bookshop. She called me on the phone one day, saying she had read my book and believed we had some similar experiences. She asked if we could meet.

That meeting was the beginning of our relationship as colleagues and friends. Unlike Lyn, I had never been diagnosed with dissociative identity disorder (which at the time was known as multiple personality disorder), but I was highly dissociative, having mastered the art of leaving my body during times of extreme pain. Huge chunks of my childhood were simply blank, and the excruciating excavation I undertook during years of therapy eventually unearthed enough fragments of cognitive memory to stitch together the narrative of my childhood.

This was not the case with Lyn and is not the reality for many dissociative survivors. We buy into the myth, despite evidence to the contrary in the field of trauma and in our own bodies, that what happened was not real unless we have cognitive validation. Lyn's skill as a narrator of her internal systems of various personalities illustrates what Dr. Judith Herman, a leading Harvard psychiatrist and author of the landmark book *Trauma and Recovery* (1992,1997 Basic Books), described as *doublethink* in which, even with amnesia, people who have experienced repeated childhood trauma from which there was no escape will describe simultaneously knowing and not knowing what happened. Remembering and not remembering.

Rosie, a tiny child whose core characteristic was trust and around whom Lyn's system revolved, said that even when "he" hurt her, she would crawl back onto his lap and trust again. Rosie never revealed who the "he" was, and for years Lyn resisted believing that Rosie was any more than a figment of her imagination, even as the evidence stacked up all around her. Rosie remembers who hurt her, but Lyn does not.

Snake, a personality whose job was to slither into people Lyn began to trust and dissect their true intentions, claimed to have been created in the moment of the first penetration and fled the body to escape the searing pain of rape. Visceral, cunning, and sly, he did not care if Lyn died, because he abided in a realm outside of her body. Snake held rage and was devoted to protecting Lyn's children, ready to shoot venom into anyone that would harm them. Snake knew about the rape so Lyn would not know.

In this book, you'll meet more than ten distinct personalities who began to surface when Lyn was in her mid-thirties, happily married and mothering four young children in a yellow-brick house in a leafy suburban community. She had no conscious memory of having been abused as a child, but during the firestorm of betrayal and upheaval when her husband admitted and then defended his infidelity, the internal walls that kept the trauma-formed personalities hidden from her awareness began to crack, the fissures resulting in a bewildering array of voices with divergent thoughts and emotions, held loosely in check by an exhausted mediator who was trying to keep the internal family functioning while Lyn's own family was falling apart.

Over ten years, her family would disintegrate as Lyn fiercely struggled to understand what was happening to her and tried her best to parent her children in increasingly difficult financial and emotional circumstances. With heartbreaking courage, she writes: "*Each of us would leave the yellow-brick house, one by one, broken, just a shadow of who we thought we were. And it was all my fault.*"

As the founder of a nonprofit organization dedicated to preventing child sexual abuse and offering collective healing journeys for survivors, I can say without hesitation that this is a life-changing book—for survivors, for those who love them, and for anyone who wants to educate themselves on trauma-induced dissociation, particularly its manifestation as DID. Unlike the dramatic renderings of multiple personalities depicted by Hollywood, survivors with varying degrees of dissociation and DID are all around us. We are mothers, teachers, professors, therapists, pastors, and business executives. It is a real miracle that we have survived, largely in part to our ability to dissociate under extreme duress. Our bodies and minds remember—even when we don't.

LINDA CROCKETT
Director, Safe Communities
www.safecommunitiespa.org
May 29, 2021

CAST OF CHARACTERS

(AKA ALTERS, INSIDERS, OR PARTS)

Me

Rosie, the center of my system, the three-year-old who trusted over and over again.

Nanny, the one who took care of Rosie and held her physical bodily sensations of abuse.

Little Lynn, the young girl who loved her parents and was sure they loved her.

Laura, the mother, who adored children and loved mothering her real children.

Paula, the fine thinker, who turned Laura's love of children into a professional career as a teacher and administrator.

Sylvia, the teenage twin of Mike, who was lively and happy, and held the sexuality and sensuality.

Mike, the teenage twin of Sylvia, whose anger drove my entire system towards healing.

Victim, one of the first parts to make him/herself known, an amalgam of all my victimized parts before I was ready to know each individually.

Survivor, another early part, who took over and functioned well when others were unable to cope.

Protector, a God-like presence who claimed to have been there from the beginning, creating alters for me as the abuse became too hard to handle.

The Black Knight, who chopped off people's heads, by ending relationships that appeared dangerous to the system.

No Name, who lived in a tunnel and held the box of memories, securely closed.

Snake, who claimed to be out of body, the only alter who did not give a hoot about me but loved my real children and wanted to protect them with the wiles of a serpent.

Devil, a shapeless glob of shame located in the center of my chest; Rosie's dark-side alter.

And others not named . . .

PART 1
Coming Undone

1981–1991

Coming Undone

I am beginning to wonder if I am crazy, if the world I know is real.
I am beginning to doubt my own perception of reality. I am very confused.
My thinking and feeling don't match. I have to rely on my thinking
mode because my feeling mode is too painful. Then when things get
stressful my thinking gives way
and I <u>have</u> to rely on my feelings and that is too painful.
Every time someone or something hurts me, it is affirmation of
my worthlessness.
Last week I saw my face in a restaurant mirror, and I was dead.
It was my dead face.

I feel like something is just beneath the surface,
something frightening, ready to hatch out.

And I know what it is:
<u>Nothing</u>

Nothing is there, no one hurt me.
I am just like this because I am either worthless or insane.
If I can fall completely into my feelings, then maybe I can let go. Maybe
I can die.

April 1991

3

CHAPTER 1

WHEN THE BUBBLE BURST

It was somewhere between my thirty-fourth and thirty-ninth year when I began to go crazy. It's hard to remember the exact date. Things moved from great to awful in small increments. My sense of being real to becoming unreal came in wisps and snatches. My love for my children consumed me until one day I lost it. I looked everywhere but couldn't find it. I always thought I was sane until I wasn't, and then I was crazy. Or at least I thought I was.

In the beginning, though, we were happy. My husband, John, our three children, and I had just moved into our new home in a small suburban Philadelphia town, and everyone was excited to be closer to our extended family. The house was three stories high with a yellow-brick facade and an oversized, fenced-in backyard. I loved the curly, twisty branches of the Japanese red maple tree that framed the turn-of-the-twentieth-century architecture. It was graceful and called to be climbed. A crook in the trunk branched into several mid-sized limbs where my children used to sit or hide or magically transform the tree into an old Western fort. We were the perfect family, and I was the perfect wife and mother who had found my calling in taking care of my brood.

John was writing his PhD dissertation in sociology, so we designated the attic room at the top of a narrow flight of stairs in the yellow-brick house as his office. He was the breadwinner who engaged his academic career in the traditional classroom and while drinking beer in bars where he said students were more relaxed and open to deeper discussions. Teaching with an informal flair, his trademark was casual attire and old, loose-fitting khakis.

Life was good. Things changed. Over the next ten years, our family would disintegrate. Each of us would leave the yellow-brick house, one by one, broken, just a shadow of who we thought we were. And it was all my fault.

⁌

My eight-year-old daughter, Lizzy, barreled through the kitchen, grabbing a granola bar in one hand and balancing her bundle of baseball cards in the other, a whirl of energy advancing through the house on her way to the backyard to meet her friends. We were settled into our new home and getting down to the business of being family in a new environment. No doubt about it, Lizzy was a tomboy. Her silver-tongued negotiations would eventually yield her the best stack of players among her male peers. Steve Carleton? Pete Rose? It mattered little to them that the Phillies were having their worst season ever. Sprawled across the grass early on a sunny summer morning, she huddled with three neighborhood boys, examining, critiquing, and comparing their cards to figure out their next trades.

"Don't get mud on your new jeans," I yelled to my oldest daughter through the backdoor screen. All morning, the fast friends would hop up and disappear into someone else's house only to reappear in our yard in the next thirty minutes or so, repeating the ritual over and over again.

In the meantime, two-year-old Chuckie finished his Cheerios, slid down from the table, and toddled outside to the sandbox. From a distance, I saw the sand slip through his fingers, then saw the inevitable hurricane of teeny-tiny stone particles flying around the yard, here, there, and everywhere. Bored after a few minutes, he waddled over to his sister, and fell *kerplop* on her back.

"Hey, get off me, you little oaf!" Lizzy laughed as she grabbed Chuckie in a bear hug. After a wrestle on the grass, Lizzy went back to her cards and Chuckie went off to throw the ball to Trixie, the mangy mid-sized pup who had adopted us not long after we moved into our pet-friendly home.

I watched them out the kitchen window and took pleasure in seeing how much fun they were having. In the back of my mind, I knew someone was missing. *Where's Kimmy?* I had seen my five-year-old daughter reading in bed, so I knew she was awake, but she hadn't made it down to the land of the living. I walked to the second floor and peered around the corner and up the steep steps to the third floor. My husband's office door was ajar. An early reader, sometimes Kimmy liked to sneak up and hide among the books and maps and atlases and other grown-up learning tools John had accumulated over the years. Sure enough, when I walked the next flight of stairs, there she was, sprawled across the small twin bed squeezed in between the large office desk and floor-to-ceiling shelves. Surrounded by books, each representing her burgeoning list of passions, she sat there intently examining the globe.

"Mommy, Mommy, look what I found," she blurted out, thrusting the colorful orb in front of me so I would discover, too, some country or continent she hadn't known existed. I smiled and sat down next to her, sharing her exuberance and taking note of the fact that she hadn't eaten breakfast yet.

"That's terrific, Kimmy," I said, giving her a hug. "Maybe we can do some research on the country later today. But for now, let's get downstairs and have breakfast!"

The morning rolled on with everyone doing what you might expect of a family of three active children. Our lives were built around playing games, building castles in the sand, reading books, acting out stories, making gingerbread houses, going hiking, accumulating pets, dancing to the music, and creating the scariest haunted houses on Halloween. The children were living their own unique lives, but I was in the center, the connector, the lover, the wiper-of-noses, the hugger, the organizer, the mother. This was our family portrait, frozen in time, the best of the best, real and not posed, or so it seemed to me.

Over the next five years, our family transformed slowly from Norman Rockwell's quintessential portrait in the *Saturday Evening Post* to Edvard Munch's existential angst in his painting *The Scream*. Although each of us remained a unique piece in the puzzle that was our family, the pieces were no longer aligned. I couldn't find a way to make their edges fit, no matter how hard I tried. Here I was, the master puzzle maker, who could no longer make sense of the picture I had created. I lost my sense of self. If I was no longer the lover of all things that had to do with my children, then who was I?

"Lizzy, do your homework before you go out with friends," I said like a hiker attempting a steep climb I had faced before. I knew my rebellious thirteen-year-old daughter would ignore me and leave her essay behind. *If only John were home to help with the discipline*, I thought. I was overwhelmed that Lizzy was testing me and John was AWOL in co-parenting. I didn't, at the time, understand that being overwhelmed was a cover for being angry, an emotion I barely knew existed and would never allow myself to feel. The door slammed as Lizzy stomped outside. I pivoted to Kimmy, who was sitting at our round oak table and needed help with her fourth-grade math homework. Her wavy blond hair looked pretty, but her bangs needed trimming.

"Let's see. This is how you set up your long division problem, Kim," I said, eyeing tears of frustration trickling down her cheeks through stray curls.

The afternoon had been packed with soccer practice for all of the kids. Lizzy excelled in soccer and left her classmates in the dust. Kimmy acquiesced to the sport even though she would have preferred to stay home and read a book. Chuckie couldn't wait to get out on the field and fly as fast as his feet would let him. After practice, I brought them home, told them to wash up, and made dinner for my motley crew, who seemed to think that grabbing the ketchup and mustard from each other was another form of soccer they could play at the kitchen table.

Lizzy snatched her food and refused to sit with the rest of us. Still more at ease with her local guy friends, who now appreciated her long brown hair, curvy body, and wide, infectious smile, she had turned moody with the family. John's seat at the table was perpetually empty because he was still at school, teaching or talking or reading or otherwise doing what academics do. By now, this was our modus operandi, and I was accustomed to not having him around. I had taken an early childhood elementary-teaching position two years earlier, and my lesson plans sat untouched in the tote bag I had thrown in the corner of the dining room.

"I don't wanna do homework," yelled Chuckie, who was cycling through second grade. His sandy red hair was tousled as he gulped down his dinner and ran upstairs to hide in his closet with his superhero dolls. My favorite childhood picture of him showed his lower lip in a noticeable pout, his streak of stubbornness on full display. I turned back and looked at Kimmy, who was always content to keep her nose in a book. With her lively blue eyes, she seemed perpetually good natured, always agreeable, always engaged with school and books in her quiet, introverted way. Just three years younger than Lizzy, their dispositions couldn't be more different.

The trials I experienced in parenting began much like they do for all families, but there was something more I couldn't quite put my finger on. Something confusing. Something that didn't make sense and was just out of my reach. *I'm exhausted,* I thought. *I can barely move. No, I'm doing great. Just get it all organized at home the way you do at school, and the problems will disappear. Are you kidding? Problems don't disappear. Just pull it together the way you manage school. You're great there. No, I have to go to sleep. Where's John? I have to keep it together for John. Nobody seems happy anymore. Well, I can tell you right now, I'm not happy. Yes, I am. What's going on? Every part of my body hurts. I'm always happy. Ha! You're delusional. Let's go to sleep. I'm scared.*

One Saturday morning, I dragged myself out of our marital bed, which had seen less and less of John and I together in the past year or so, and confronted my husband at the bathroom door. Early bird that he was, he had already had two cups of coffee at a local diner and came home just as the rest of us were waking up. I had sleepers in my eyes. "Have you ever had an affair?"

Where did this question come from? I wondered as the words popped out of my mouth. In less than an instant, a myriad of thoughts flew through my mind. *Of course John's faithful. Why would you ask that question? He's a good man and he loves us. He's our whole life and we're a family. He would never cheat on me. You are so naïve. He's never around. You don't see half the things that go on, and your life is falling apart. Why not ask? How do you expect he'll answer? How do you want him to answer? Do I care?* I hid a yawn and waited impatiently for him to respond.

"Yes," he said, barely audible, gazing down at the worn rug, the smell of fresh coffee still clinging to his stretched-out, holey sweater.

Some part of me heard him without an ounce of feeling. As animated and loving as I had been in the past, this lack of feeling was becoming more and more familiar to me. Instead, I was curious, cold, analytical, with just a hint of panic. "When?"

"Now."

"How long?"

"Two years." His hazel-green eyes reconnected with mine. They seemed to be trying to tell me something. Maybe he was sorry? Maybe he felt guilty? Maybe he wanted me to forgive and forget? His body relaxed like the taut frame of the wild goose flying, felled with one shot.

I, on the other hand, was the bullet ready to take flight. I didn't wait to find out what he was trying to communicate. In an act of agency and symbolism, I grabbed my antidepressant medication and threw it down the toilet. *Yes, I'm depressed. Yes, I've thought it's a sign of my own weakness. But, yes, there is a reason. He's been having an affair for two years. I'm getting out of here.*

With a final glance, I told John I was going to my parents' apartment an hour away and walked quickly out the door. Driving blindly, I passed cars along the turnpike, zigzagged across Lancaster Avenue, and watched side street after side street disappear through my rearview mirror. With little memory of how I got wherever I was going or what I thought along the way, my whole body, mind, and spirit were activated into survival mode, and the luxury of thinking through implications seemed unavailable to me. Instead, the back of my brain was filled with silver, shimmering icicles, the kind that enthralled me when I was a little girl, icicles swaying on my Christmas tree, preventing any trace of coherent thought. I would later learn this was my body's response to trauma, a sign of *dissociation*, the psychological term used to describe the state of experiencing oneself and one's surroundings as unreal, and often the compartmentalizing of pain, fear, and functioning. Out of my *fight, flight, or freeze* options, I had chosen flight.

Eventually, I found myself in the blue-collar neighborhood of my upbringing and slid my car next to the curb in front of my parents' second-floor apartment. Cattycorner to the building, the lights of the ice and coal company flashed. Down the street, the taproom was getting ready for lunch. Directly across the street, the busy beer distributor of my childhood was boarded up and silent like a morgue. I walked past trash cans to the front door and dragged myself up the familiar stairwell, rubbing my hands along the sturdy pine railing as I went, step by step. Once at the top of the landing, I found my way to my childhood bedroom and crawled into my bed where the faded blue bedspread with worn-out tufts was draped across its frame. I wrapped it around me, pulled my knees to my chin, and closed my eyes. The adrenaline was wearing thin, and my real circumstances began to take shape. Now I was the felled goose, limp and loose and totally unsure of who I was or what I was supposed to do. The world had turned on a dime.

My mother and father stood over me curled up in my cocoon as I croaked out the story. My mother tried to console me. My father just looked at me and said, "He never should have told you."

Then he walked away.

My father never was the warm and fuzzy sort.

An electrician by trade, the "old fart," as he called himself, grumbled and grunted through his spectacles, rarely smiled, and laughed even less. His almost bald head gleamed like a crown atop his khaki shirt and pants, the uniform he wore to his job as a bank maintenance superintendent and carried over at home and even in retirement. Save some extra wrinkles, his sculpted face and nose changed little over my lifetime and commanded the same obedience from his beginning to his end.

"People who believe in God are either stupid or weak," he had pronounced as an article of faith around the dinner table set precisely for his six o'clock meal, or on the back porch overlooking our dingy alley as he lit up a cigarette, or with my sister and the friends she brought home from college. He made sure we all knew his disdain for religion that, in his mind, was a crutch that upheld the masses, a holdover idea, perhaps, from his days in post-war New York City with communist and socialist friends.

"If you can't see, hear, taste, touch, or feel it, it doesn't exist" was another commandment he threw around as he flicked his ashes into a dirty ashtray. It made sense to me. I couldn't imagine an imaginary man in the sky who, like Santa Claus, knew what everyone needed all around the world all at once. It sounded preposterous. I didn't like the mean words my father used to describe religious people, but I had to agree that he made sense. After all, for small children, their parents are God, of a sort, and my father had become a God-like figure for me, endowed with supreme authority as well as the capacity for ultimate retribution. Just as many people dare not cross the God of their imagining, I dared not cross my father.

Still, I always longed for God. From as far back as I can remember, I sensed a presence. While I couldn't imagine an old man in the sky, I felt a deep sense of something more. I knew enough not to call this presence God, but it was real.

We were a socially isolated family amid a sea of people. Beneath us, next to us, down the block, and across the street were folks we rubbed shoulders with, but we were different. They had family rituals; we didn't. They went on vacations; we didn't. They went to church; we didn't. They had friends; we didn't. So, in order to make us moderately normal and minimally acceptable, my mother sent my sister and me to the red-brick Methodist church a block away from our house so we would know what other people knew even though we didn't believe what other people believed. My sister lasted for one service, but I took to it handily and became a regular at Sunday school from first to fifth grade. I sang in the children's choir. I memorized twelve Bible verses a week for twelve weeks to earn a free week at a summer church camp. I was confirmed. I didn't know how to believe in God, but I was happy to drink the Kool-Aid.

By chance, when I entered junior high school, I stumbled upon *Being and Nothingness* by the French existentialist Jean Paul Sartre. I devoured the work of this great mind who seemed to have an understanding of the world far beyond my grasp. I was taken by his notion that people must claim their own destiny rather than rely on a God to give meaning to their lives. The idea of individual responsibility for oneself and others was similar to what I learned at church, but it lived outside the need for a pretend deity whose existence was unprovable. Sartre's philosophy fit neatly within my father's worldview, and I loved the notion that I could make meaning for my own life. Still, existentialism didn't address the small stirrings in my heart. Did these stirrings come from my Sunday school classes? Did they exist in me independently? If I tried, maybe I could ignore them. So, at the age of thirteen, I stuffed my spirituality, walked out the door of the red-brick Methodist church, and didn't look back. I would be an atheist, just like my father. Like Sartre, I would make meaning for myself.

John was an ex-Catholic, ex-altar boy who was also an atheist. I met him at Temple University in Philadelphia where he was a graduate student in sociology and I was an underclassman. Five minutes late on my way to class, I was rushing up the stairs of Gladfelter Hall as, at the exact same moment, he descended with his head in a book. Two karmic bodies collided, and the contents of our arms scattered everywhere. As we both leaned over to collect our collateral, our eyes met.

"Oh, I'm so sorry," I said as I picked up two books.

"No, it was my fault," he replied as he gathered three of his own and a bunch of papers. We slowly stood upright, and I got a good look at him. He was cute and his eyes twinkled. Even better, he didn't make me nervous. "Would you like to have lunch at the Grill after class?" he asked like a pup waiting for a treat. Usually, I had extreme anxiety around men my age, which had severely limited my social life. Trembling lips and brain freeze had never made me queen of the ball. The dancing icicles in my brain would form an impermeable wall between me and any would-be suitor. But John didn't do that to me. For some reason, I could talk to him without getting panicky. We caught lunch and were both besmitten. One thing led to another, and we eloped six months later.

John and I shared the same values. We were both atheists, which was its own kind of religion. That did us well for a good part of our marriage, but toward its end, I became uncomfortable with his approach to teaching students how religion interfaced with culture. College is intended to stretch and challenge the worldviews of students, and John approached this task with a fervor that went beyond basic academic responsibility. He seemed to take pleasure in undermining the convictions of students who came to his class with a deep faith.

One cold winter afternoon, John was driving carefully through the snow patches while I sat in the passenger seat, working on a list of things to buy at the supermarket. The conversation was idle until he replayed his day. "My sociology of religion class is going well," he said. "Today, one of my students raised some issues after my lecture. I dismantled his beliefs pretty quickly." He chuckled heartily, giving details of the classroom conversation as he steered the car through a slide. "I nearly brought him to the point of tears. Religion is so illogical. He's a bright boy. I can't believe he would believe such things," he said with a sense of satisfaction that he had accomplished what he had set out to do.

I watched the bright-white landscape pass dreamily by and realized John's story made me uncomfortable. It seemed to me that stretching a student's mind to grow was one thing, but bringing a student to the point of tears and enjoying it was quite another. I was an atheist too, but the gleam in his eye and the laughter in his voice was unsettling. We moved on to other topics as we went shopping, then returned home and unpacked our bags. Perhaps for the first time in our marriage, I carried my discomfort with me.

When I married John, I thought I was choosing the polar opposite of my father. He seemed like an upbeat, expressive sort of guy, so different from the grouchy, untouchable person whose genes I carried. I've heard it said that we unconsciously choose a new version of our parent for our spouse, but I remember thinking, *Not me. I didn't fall into that trap.*

My emergency response to John's admission of infidelity slowly dissipated, but it left my body numb, exhausted, yet still in high alert. Like a soldier in jungle combat, I knew the immediate danger had passed, but the hostile environment hid unknown perils that might flare up at any moment. After a dreamless sleep and breakfast at my parents' kitchen table, I got into my car and drove slowly home. My children needed me even though I was becoming less effective in parenting by the day. My school was waiting for me, oblivious to what was unfolding behind our closed doors. My husband was anxious for my return in hopes I would forget about his transgression. I would face the unknown dangers ahead. I was afraid, but I would walk through the jungle anyway. What choice did I have?

CHAPTER 2

BEFORE THE BURST

I began to show signs of losing my mind before the bubble burst. Fear and shame had left their marks on my happy life in spite of my best efforts to push them down, shove them away, and pretend them out of existence.

At the age of thirty-five, I went to graduate school for a master's degree in education and teaching certification. Many years prior, I had opened a little nursery school in my home when Lizzy was three. I had taught in Head Start when she was four. I took a second-to-third grade teaching position at an international school in Spain when she was six. All this without any training in teaching. Perhaps I could reshape the love I had for my children and channel it into a classroom. John supported this career move and agreed to watch our brood while I went to school. I would become a teacher.

My grand plans were almost stopped in their tracks by my first student-teaching experience. An integral conclusion to the graduate program, student teaching meant putting our ideas to the test in a real classroom under the supervision of an experienced teacher. In my case, I would spend the first ten weeks in first grade and the second ten weeks in fifth grade.

I was intimidated by my supervising first-grade teacher. I thought I was supposed to be like her, but I was not like her. Her short hair styled with tight curls was never out of place, and she wore dark skirts and professional blouses, so different from my relaxed and casual look, a euphemism for wrinkled clothing and hair that never stayed put. Younger than me, she was small but authoritative, and as assertive as I was unsure of myself. I rarely saw her show warmth to the children under her care. The biggest giveaway, though, was the way she arranged her class with twenty-five desks all in neat rows.

"I'd like to try some experiential learning with the children in science class. Look at these experiments. They can work on them in small groups at their desks," I proposed. My experience in early-childhood classes and in the elementary school in Spain had given me the opportunity to work with children in child-centered classrooms immersed in hands-on learning. I imagined the children scouting for rocks at home, bringing them into the classroom, sorting through them together, keeping charts on the types of rocks they had found, and labeling pictures with invented spelling as records of the colors, textures, and weights of formations that could be found in our neighborhood.

"That will never work," she replied, looking down her nose at me with an air of disdain. "Here, these are the worksheets I use when I'm teaching that unit." She shoved a bunch of papers into my hand. "Keep the students in their desks and keep order in the room."

I was crushed. Worksheets were the antithesis of how I thought children learned. All my confidence flew out the window when my supervising teacher shot down every new idea I suggested. Instead of pressing on, I let her strip me of my sense of worth. I didn't realize at the time, but this was the first trigger that began to peel away my outer layer of self. When I was in her presence, shame washed over me. When I tried to communicate my teaching plans, my mind froze in fear. When she looked at me with contempt, my body spasmed in pain. Visions of icicles came and went each morning when I walked into the classroom, and each afternoon when I packed up to go home. *Whatever made me think I could be a teacher?* I asked myself. *I'm a terrible teacher. No, I'm a good teacher. You're a good teacher. No, I'm not. Just listen to my supervisor. I don't belong here. She's the boss. She knows I'm a fake.*

My supervising teacher's demeanor and my emotional and physical response was not a figment of my imagination. When I moved to the fifth-grade classroom, the new supervising teacher said, "I don't know what happened to you on the elementary wing, but put that out of your head and plan to have an excellent experience with me." I did. Still, my sense of safety had been badly shaken, and it took time for my body and mind to recover. I graduated and earned my teaching certification that year with trepidation.

A year later, I learned that several local women and men were forming a Quaker elementary school. Two realities played tug-of-war in my mind: *I'm a fake. I can't manage a classroom. Why would you even think of applying? No, you're a talented teacher. You'd be perfect for this job.* The part of me who thought I had gifts in teaching won the argument, and I decided to apply. The vision for the Quaker school was a child-centered curriculum, creative teaching strategies, and a gentle spiritual foundation. It was right up my alley. *Maybe I can put the past behind me. Maybe student teaching was a bad dream. Maybe I can discover I really am the teacher I thought I was.*

After the parents interviewed me three times, I sensed they were going to offer me the job, so I thought I'd better be honest. "I've really enjoyed interviewing with you and meeting your kids," I said as I rose from my position on the floor in a church basement. I had been teaching their children a sample lesson as part of the interview. "I share your vision. I hope you will offer me the position. But I think it's only fair to tell you I'm an atheist. I don't believe in God," I confessed with a lump in my throat. Without hesitation, the parents, who would also serve as future school administrators, joined together in reassuring me.

"That's not a problem. You have the qualities we're looking for," said one of the mothers whose little boy would attend the school.

"You have a unique spirituality," said another whose daughter was on the class list.

"You relate well to our children, and you're creative in your approach," said a father who would become one of the first board members.

Apparently, the parents saw something in me that I didn't see myself because they offered me the position.

Over the course of the next year, we advertised and held several open houses where I provided hands-on activities for the children who attended and an educational talk describing our proposed curriculum for their parents. "Sign me on!" said one mother. Her daughter became one of our first students. The family had no ties with Quakers, but she thought our approach sounded perfect.

"I want my two sons to attend," said another mother who was a Quaker. She was looking for a school with a set of values that matched her own. One boy would be a kindergartener and one a second grader.

The enrollments kept coming, and I was gratified. It was an affirmation that these parents respected what I had to offer their children. They didn't want worksheets; they wanted real hands-on learning and a sense their children would be growing in empathy, compassion, and action. *I always knew I was a good teacher,* I told myself. *Why didn't I know that when I was student teaching? It's like I'm two different people. I know what I'm doing now. I have confidence now. They like what I'm doing.*

The excitement of being affirmed in my teaching was balanced by caution. *How will it work at home when teaching? Your family isn't used to that. Lots of mothers work when their children are young. Why shouldn't I work? That's what I went to school for. Okay. We'll give it a try. Let's see how it goes. It's safe. I'm safe. Be careful.* I was excited and glad to be given another chance to do what I felt in my bones I was supposed to do, but a heaviness that came from nowhere haunted me.

I didn't feel crazy in the classroom. "There's 'that of God' in every person, in every one of you sitting here today, and in everyone everywhere all over the world," I told the children sitting around me on the floor. This was the underlying Quaker belief I was expected to teach the fifteen kindergarten-to-third-grade students in the Quaker school where I taught. It was three years after we had moved to the yellow-brick house and the first year of the school's existence. At the age of thirty-seven, I had been entrusted with the school's one and only multi-graded class.

On this particular morning, kids buzzed around in intentional chaos organized by our task chart that told everyone what they were supposed to do. The cheerful light of the sky-blue walls on the second floor of a local church helped set the tone. Some of the children had plopped down on beanbag chairs to read their favorite books in a quiet alcove set up for exploring award-winning kid literature. Another group worked together on a science project in a smaller alcove in the large, spacious room. The youngest kids were building with blocks, while another group was working at tables on math problems. Each morning culminated in writers' workshop where all the children wrote and illustrated their stories. Just before lunch, we gathered under the bulletin board for our daily meeting for worship combining a little bit of silence and a lot of values clarification. It was a giggly morning.

"What do you think that means about you?" I asked, referring to the one-and-only Quaker doctrine of God-within. I wanted the kids to use their five, six, seven, and eight-year-old logic to explore and consider how it might impact the way they moved in the world. They were squirmy.

"It means God must love me and you, too," said a little girl with red pigtails who was sitting up straight and grinning at me. Tacked on the bulletin board was a poster with children's hands in all shades of color, clasped together like the spokes of a wheel. Around it were examples of their first attempts at writing. Someone crawled from one side of our group circle to another, bumping into other kids along the way.

"What does that mean about your neighbor—the one you like, and the one you don't like?" I pushed the class a little further, giving the small traveler in our midst a kind and gentle version of my evil eye. Quakers, formally known as the Religious Society of Friends, worshiped God by sitting in meditative silence for an hour each week and applied their faith through peace, education, simplicity, and other testimonies that reflected their beliefs. They were known for justice activism that grew out of silent meditation and called their weekly church services "meetings."

"Oh, I guess that means we have to be nice to people even if we don't like them. Because God is inside of them," said a little boy who was rolling around on the floor. I snapped my fingers and he popped up quickly and sat erect in his spot next to me.

"Does it give you any other clues about how to treat someone else?" I asked my tribe of wigglers. A little girl with long blond hair squealed when the boy next to her accidentally pushed her as he grabbed for some apples that had fallen out of his pocket. I could smell the peanut butter on his sweater left over from snack. There was an apple stain on the rug where his knee had mashed into the fabric.

"I guess we have to go out of our way to talk to people when we don't agree with them so we can learn how to get along," said one of the more mature boys, who would turn out to be a leader. After a little more serious discussion, we all broke down and laughed. "That of God" was calling us into fun.

Silliness or not, our conversations were illuminating, especially for me. I believed there was something special in every person, so using the language of Quakers was an easy stretch. By the end of the first year at the school, I realized the God words felt honest. They felt right. I still didn't believe in God, but I felt comfortable with how the God-that-didn't-exist was using me.

At the age of thirty-eight, I had begun to attend the historic stone Quaker meetinghouse just a few blocks from my house. Life was getting more complicated in my home and in my head. Maybe I could find peace with these people who practiced their faith not by singing, speaking, or praising, but by silence. Tentative but clearly drawn, I found myself in a community I had never experienced. I learned that Quakers imagined the divine as some sort of permutation between silence and light, and they "held you in the light" if you needed what other traditions called prayer. The concept of light appealed to me. Like most of us when we are confronted with a theological concept, I didn't know what it meant, but it felt real and far more accessible than an old man in the sky.

Most important, I discovered a depth of healing while sitting in the hour of silence at Quaker meetings for worship. The silence didn't take away my craziness, but it gave me a respite. Settled on the old wooden benches next to unadorned plaster walls, each of the twenty or thirty worshipers were literally called out of our own worlds and into a liminal space.

I was broken. I was hurting. I was dark. *I need faith,* I wrote in my journal, describing my experience of the Quaker meeting. The silence held me safely as I drifted from thought to no thought, from suffering to suspension, from pain to sanctuary. *I believe faith is a part of the fabric of my being which I have denied for so long.*

I hungered, imagining what I had yet to know. *I wish my faith were deeper,* I prayed. *I want what all these other worshipers have.*

Apart yet together, imperceptibly, the presence gathered us in.

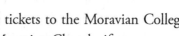

"I have some tickets to the Moravian College Christmas Vespers held at Central Moravian Church, if anyone wants them," a woman wearing a bright-red sweater and a green scarf announced at the close of our Quaker meeting for worship one early December morning, just a few months before I would learn of John's affair. It was customary for members to rise and make announcements before disbanding for coffee and sweet cake. I had been attending Quaker meetings for about a year, the only one of my family to do so—still an atheist, but yearning for a presence beyond my grasp. "Just see me during fellowship." She smiled, her cheeks wide and rosy.

"Oh, I'd love the tickets," I exclaimed when I bumped into her in the crowd. "I've never been, and maybe my mother would want to go with me this year." This well-loved service drew people of all faiths and backgrounds from a wide geographic area, so the church required worshipers to have tickets—free for the asking—in order to attend.

My parents would be visiting during the holidays. My mother was not an atheist like my father; she was an agnostic, which matched her gentler manner and softer style. She had taught me a few church hymns in my youth, so she must have heard the church bells ring sometime in her history. In spite of her doubt, she didn't try to keep me from experiencing the symbols of faith, especially during major holidays. We bundled up and made the nighttime pilgrimage to the church, leaving John and my father to watch the children.

Bethlehem, Pennsylvania was known far and wide as the Christmas City. We parked the car and breathed in the holiday. The sounds of "O Little Town of Bethlehem" poured out of speakers mounted high on every corner. The streets were strung with lights, and each lamppost was adorned with an evergreen wreath tied with an exquisite red bow. Shops bustled with customers examining carefully the artisan wares, elegant clothing, handcrafted furniture, books, pottery, and pretty much anything you might have hoped for. On the hour, every hour, a cluster of carolers gathered under an enormous lit Christmas tree to sing the classic carols.

My mother and I made our way through the crowds and walked up the steps of the plain Federal-style building where a tall, dignified gentleman with a red bow tie greeted us.

"Merry Christmas," he said in a kind voice, "and welcome to Central Moravian Church." We handed him our tickets, and he pointed us toward the stairwell where we were subsumed into a sea of people making their way to the balcony. From this vantage, we were able to look down on the worship space and gain the wide expanse of plain interior with elegantly appointed decorations: perfectly handmade wreathes, bright-red poinsettias, a carefully crafted putz—the Moravian term for creche—in the center of the church chancel. Baby Jesus was asleep in the manger. Just below us sat the large choir and a potpourri of musicians. People milled around, finding their seats and greeting old friends.

Like aliens in a strange land, my mother and I sat quietly, uncertain of what to expect, waiting with anticipation for the service to begin. The lights dimmed. The congregation hushed. Ancient music filled the sanctuary. Music, word, light, drama—the service unfolded. In the midst of my deep darkness, the Christmas story inspired me with awe. I sat captivated, fully invested in what was unfolding. Suddenly, midway through the service, a young boy's unchanged soprano voice quivered through the air with the lyrics of the traditional hymn "Morning Star."

Morning Star, O cheering sight!
Ere though cam'st, how dark earth's night!
Jesus mine, in me shine; in me shine, Jesus mine;
fill my heart with light divine.

I sat still, mesmerized, letting his fragile voice penetrate my outward facade and touch something deep inside me, ready to be set free. There was wisdom in this boy's voice, even though he couldn't have been older than eleven or twelve. Did he understand what he was singing, really understand it? His thin, undeveloped body was young yet carried the weight of authority by virtue of this classic carol. He was singing some sort of truth that was hard to comprehend. *He's a child, just a child,* I thought in envy and awe. *Yet he knows something I don't know.* Tentatively, a part of me emerged and said, *I'm a child too. I'm just like him but even younger. You can trust him because he knows what all of us children know—that the God-that-doesn't-exist loves us.* No wonder Christmas was a happy holiday. *Someone loves us.*

The lyrics brought me to my knees—a cry against dark earth's night. Dark earth's night? That meant it wasn't just me who was feeling the darkness; other people were too. This whole church must feel the darkness because they were singing about it. Not only that, but this hymn wasn't depressing. It was hopeful. A morning star, a Christ figure, and a light divine—all these seemed to be an antidote to darkness. *I want to cry.* I couldn't formulate words because the feelings were so profound. I was aware, instead, of words I couldn't articulate, of feelings that were new. *I can't manage anything. I'm always hurting, always sad, always afraid, and, most of all, never me. I'm never me anymore. Here I am, sitting in church, and I hear that I don't have to be me. God loves me whoever I am. This Christ figure will take care of me. I will be okay.*

Water welled up in my eyes. I felt shifts in my body and movement in my mind as I tried to integrate this experience of what I would later call God but, in the moment, had no words for. The experience wasn't frightening, it wasn't confusing, but it wasn't clear either. I didn't know what it meant or where it would take me, but it was an intimate invitation to me, Lyn, to trust that I was loved and would be alright. I discovered on that night that I didn't have to believe in anything in particular to participate in the healing, life-giving act of worship. I just had to surrender.

Like Quaker meeting, the Christmas Vespers embodied light and brought me face-to-face with the "light that shines in the darkness" that "the darkness did not overcome" (John 1:5). I was in the midst of my own darkness and I heard it. In the shadows at the end of the service, we all lifted our beeswax candles with red-curled collars high into the night to witness together that the light ultimately wins, whether we believe in the light or not.

One spring morning just months after the beautiful Christmas Vespers, I would stumble out of my bed and ask John about his faithfulness. "Have you ever had an affair?" With his answer, I would begin to grasp the vague contours of my darkness which before then had seemed inexplicable. My self-protective instincts would move from low to high alert, and I would keep constant watch, for what I did not know. A cloud of shame and fear followed me everywhere I went, covering me with shadow I couldn't escape. The mountains before me were still hidden. The only way past them would be through them.

CHAPTER 3

CHAOS

S kin. I was sure my skin was different from everyone else's. Other people had nice, smooth skin that enjoyed the sense of touch, that molded to their bodies, that held all their organs in place. My skin used to be like that. I especially loved curling up with my little babies and toddlers, skin against skin, taking naps together in the middle of the day, catching up on the sleep we missed the night before. I loved brushing their hair with the tips of my fingers, holding them on my back or my hips, feeling their arms around my neck, feeling the dribble of slobber kisses rolling lazily down my cheek, the sensations of security, the sensations of love.

Driving home from my parents' apartment after learning of John's affair, I couldn't feel my skin anymore. Instead, this outer bodily layer was like a parchment stretched over empty bones, a hollow cave. Instead of a heart, a nameless organ forced red liquid through constricted vessels. Instead of lungs expanding and contracting unnoticed, breath was shallow, a stolen commodity, never certain a next breath would crawl out from under its hiding place. I used to feel the warmth of touch like other people, but no more—another sign I was defective. Now my skin existed in two states of being: either numb or as layers of flesh, whole battalions of follicles pulsing with pain as the history of thirty or forty years began to push against the boundaries of my tissue, as my brain went into overdrive or shut down, as my emotions cascaded loop-de-loop and down, as if on a ski slope.

As I continued the drive home, the icicles in the back of my mind saved me.

After fifteen years of marriage, John didn't want a divorce, extramarital affair notwithstanding. Looking back, I suspect he had several affairs during our jaunts around the country while he was establishing himself in his career. I had been naïve not to notice. Four years into our marriage, camping from our home in the Midwest to our families on the East Coast and back again, we closed out the summer with incredible itching in our genital areas. Our doctor told us we had gonorrhea.

"How could this be? I haven't had sexual relations with anyone but you," I wondered aloud, balancing an overactive three-year-old and a nursing baby at my breast.

"I have no idea. Maybe we picked it up while we were camping," John said, and, just like that, we became the 0.01 percent that contracts venereal disease from camp toilets. I never questioned his explanation because it was easier to believe the story that fit the fantasy.

Often John would spend summers doing research on the other side of the country. On his return one year, he waited for young Lizzy and Kimmy to go to bed before telling me he wanted to talk to me about something serious. "Sure, John," I said, totally unaware of what was coming. We walked into the living room together, and he firmly closed the French doors behind us. Rebuffing the comfy couch, we sat our young, lithe bodies down on the brown shag rug. I looked at him and waited for him to begin.

"Something isn't right, Lyn. We aren't connecting," John began hesitantly. He seemed to have trouble coming up with the words, but I listened intently. Looking back, he was probably talking about sex, but he wasn't clear, and I wasn't intuitive. I loved him. I wanted to understand him. I wanted to make him happy. Somewhere in the conversation, he said, "Maybe we need to divorce," and I was dumbfounded. With great concern, I suggested we go to couple's counseling, but he wouldn't think of it. The tone changed quickly, as if all he had just said hadn't been said. "Oh, no, I'm fine. Everything is alright." The French doors opened, the conversation ended, and our lives went on. John never brought his concerns to me again. My denial was so firmly rooted that I assumed our marriage was happy for both of us.

On another occasion, after arriving back in the States from a year in Spain where John had done fieldwork, he went into an uncharacteristic depression. His mother was an active woman but a heavy smoker, and I had noticed that she had grown frailer. Worried about her health, I was afraid this was fueling John's mood.

"John, you seem so down," I observed as we sat on my parents' back porch one sultry evening. We were living temporarily at their home until we settled into a new college town a few states away. Lizzy and Kimmy were in the cramped apartment, absorbed in their play. The sun set over our two bodies hunched side by side in melancholy conversation. A dog barked in the background, like sorrowful music. "What's wrong?" I asked. In the shadows, I could tell his head was drooping further into his body as he slowly told the story.

"I'm worried, Lyn. On one of my visits into the countryside, I met a Spanish woman at a bar. We started talking and, well, one thing led to another. Honestly, we didn't actually do anything, but we got close enough that, well, maybe, I may have been infected with a venereal disease." He paused as if the air were too heavy to carry. "I feel terrible. If I did, I might have infected you—and you're carrying our third child. What have I done?" His chest heaved with silent tears.

The image of John's mother had loomed so ominously in my thoughts that hearing this confession lifted a dark cloud. I didn't know what compartment in my mind to place his betrayal, so I simply dismissed it without thinking about it. His mother was okay, and that was all that mattered. I drew him close.

"It's okay, John. It's okay. Everything will be alright." We both were tested and found negative, so indeed everything was alright. He was my husband and divorce had never been in my vocabulary. Perhaps my unconditional acceptance of that transgression convinced him I'd forgive this affair as well.

⌒

"It's you I love. Not this woman. Please, let's start over," John pleaded as we walked around the tree-lined block in our nice, middle-class neighborhood, talking intensely about our future after his admission of a two-year affair. By the time we got back to our yellow-brick house, we'd agreed to try.

I did try to put it behind me. I really did. John made herculean efforts to win me over, but it seemed that I wasn't winnable. After a lifetime of denying the telltale signs of infidelity, I didn't have the capacity to restart the engine. Often, I was nauseous and found it hard to breathe. Frequently, my body ached, and I became eerily spacey. I was either numb or experiencing what I can only describe as psychic pain, sometimes both at the same time. These were symptoms of something I didn't understand that had been stored in my body for decades.

For the first time in my life, I thought, *I'm going to put myself first.* I didn't want to hurt John; I only knew I needed to practice self-care, another word not in my vocabulary. Some place deep inside me sensed this was about survival. I felt some guilt that I couldn't find it in myself to reconcile, but I knew I wasn't going to make a new commitment to the man who had betrayed me.

I can't feel, I cried silently in a dreamlike state of consciousness. *I can't feel anything. I'm numb. I hurt. What hurts? Everything. My whole body. How can I be numb and hurt at the same time? Where are the children? What are they doing? What have I done? It's my fault. I'm to blame. I should go back with John. But I can't. I just can't. I don't trust him. It's all my fault. I'm to blame. Just roll over and die.*

John gave me a few months' time to figure things out, but after that, he got mean.

⌒

"If I'm going to break it off with this woman, I need to know you're going to stay with me," John negotiated.

"I can't promise," I said, confused that his faithfulness was contingent upon my response to his infidelity.

It seemed that John and I each had a gaping hole in our hearts that, for many years, we plugged up for the other. I don't know what caused his hole, but mine was due to an earlier betrayal. Like a key in a lock, I had to pull myself out of his cylinder in order to tend to the corrosion in my own. This left John without the key that would modulate his emotions. Swinging wildly from devotion to disdain in an effort to figure out how the new me would fit into his architecture, John alternated between love, hate, tenderness, wrath, attention, and disrespect as patterns on his wallpaper.

"Let's play tennis," he proposed, though I'd never played tennis in my life. "Let's go dancing," he suggested, though he'd always hated to dance. "Here's a gift I thought you'd like." He tried in all sorts of ways. Sadly, I could see his sincere intent, but I was no longer the key that fit the lock. I felt like I was watching him through a gauzy glass but didn't believe him. Likewise, I heard him in an echo chamber but didn't trust him. Some of this caution was well deserved, but some of it came from the creeping fog of dissociation crawling up my limbs, into my torso, and agitating my mind in a surreal painting that put everything I had ever known into question. How could I trust him when a mysterious, shadowy filter always came between us? I couldn't imagine myself with him, but I was stuck in a nether land of indecision.

"I need time and space," I said in the months after I had discovered his affair. This was hard for John. He tried to give it to me, but his timeline was very different from mine. When it became obvious that I wasn't ready for reconciliation, our relationship deteriorated at light speed into vindictive anger on John's part, and withdrawal and survival mode on mine.

Outside, the sun was shining, but inside it was dismal and gray on the day John and I sat our seven, ten, and thirteen-year-old children down to tell them we were going to live apart. No one said a word for a few minutes as they looked out the window, scratched the upholstery on the living room couch, or fidgeted with their fingers through the whole ordeal. Their own individual angst had already started to appear, and this was one more burden to place on their vulnerable psyches.

Kimmy broke the silence, saying, "I thought you two were so happy." Sadly, we said no, we weren't, there were problems, without expanding further on the subject. We walked John to the door and bid him goodbye before he drove to a rented room near his work. We were all numb. Our new lives had begun.

That night, Chuckie awoke from a fitful sleep.

"Mommy, Mommy, where's Daddy? Daddy, Daddy!" His body was shaking from head to toe, and he sobbed inconsolably. I put my arms around him, but he only became more distraught. Not knowing how to calm and ease his tremors, I lay down and wrapped my whole body around his, legs over legs to stop the convulsing, arms around arms to provide a cocoon, soothing him, telling him it would be okay, loving him with all my aching heart. Gradually, over a period of an hour or so, the sobs became sniffles, his racking body relaxed, and he fell back to sleep.

The next day I called John to tell him what had happened, hoping he would visit and spend some time with Chuckie and the rest of us for some stability and reassurance.

"So, you've put the knife in and now you're turning it to make me feel bad," he said. "Well, I won't bite. You're on your own."

I wanted to cry. I had not yet given myself permission to feel anger. Instead, my head split, and my skin crawled with emotion I wasn't able to identify. My breath was heavy, and I submitted to my powerlessness in managing family dynamics going forward. I thought John would want to know that Chuckie was upset so he could reassure him in this time of transition. I wasn't trying to make him feel guilty, but that was how he seemed to take it. I was willing to work collaboratively. Now it felt like the blame I wasn't directing toward him was circling around and landing on me.

It's not his fault, but it's not my fault, either, I thought, my body reeling from the poison of John's words. *Yes, it is your fault. You wouldn't take him back, so you deserve this. He's your husband. Go back to him. He said you're on your own, and you are. Oh, it's his fault, yes, it is. No, it isn't. It's mine. Poor Chuckie, he's caught in the middle. I can't do it by myself. It's too much. Well, you're gonna have to because you're not gonna get much from him. He hurt me when he said that, and he hurt Chuckie, too. Why wouldn't he want to know how upset Chuckie is and try to calm him? We should be together on this. Hey, he's the one who had an affair, not me. Not you. Stay away from him. He hurts. Don't touch him. You're on your own.* The icicles were on duty, shimmering between thoughts and easing the pain of the poison.

With his response, John set the tone for the next few years. Money, how to deal with our children's emotional issues, and just being civil to one another were all problematic. A therapist suggested John write letters to release his angry feelings but warned him not to send them. John wrote the letters but forgot the part about not sending them, so I got rage-filled tomes denouncing me for every possible sin. I looked at his accusations and tried to understand his position, but it always felt like he was *projecting*, the psychological term for denying qualities in oneself while attributing those same qualities to another person, or *gaslighting*, the term for manipulating another person by making them doubt their own memory, perception, or judgment.

"There was never anything you asked for in the marriage that you did not get," John wrote in one of his letters. "You placed your wants and needs above the needs of the family, just as you are doing now. No sooner had Chuck turned three years old when you pursued your career interests full time. It was an infidelity both to me and the children. My infidelity was a response to your infidelity," he concluded. In that simple statement, he absolved himself of the guilt he felt for having an affair and placed it squarely on me.

I'm so sorry I didn't meet your needs, I answered John in my mind because having a conversation with him would likely end in a shouting match. *I tried to be a good wife to you. When you expressed unhappiness so*

*many years ago, I suggested we go to counseling, but you refused and said
everything was okay. You told me you wanted me to have the children—
"barefoot and pregnant" you said, and we both laughed. I know I've failed
our kids but not because I was pursuing some career path; I honestly don't
know what's going on inside me that keeps me from being the mother I
want to be.*

*You were proud of me when I went back to school and got my master's
degree, or at least you told me you were. You even spouted some feminist
rhetoric and said you'd pick up some of the housework, but you never did.
I'm so totally exhausted by your anger that it's making me crazy. I want to
crawl into a hole and disappear. I know I made mistakes and I know you
made mistakes, but can't we put the children first? Can't we let our anger
go? You don't know this because I don't tell you, but I feel so defective. There's
something wrong with me. I just want to roll over and die. Let me die.*

≈)

"I'm going to arrange for us to go to a mediator," John said,
drawing on a recommendation from one of his colleagues during a
tension-filled phone call. The financial details of the separation were
most problematic, and John was enraged that he might have to support
a broken family.

"Great," I responded, hoping this might smooth out some of the
sandpaper we were experiencing. Mediation didn't last long when the
mediator expected John to pay child support. At the time, I held a
teaching position in the Quaker elementary school and commanded
a very small salary. A college professor's salary in those days was fairly
modest as well, yet John made almost three times my income. There
were legitimate financial issues for both of us, but John was adamant
that he would not provide child support if I would not take steps toward
reconciliation. Two years later, I would file for support legally, but until
that time, we scraped the bottom of the barrel.

Okay, I thought, *if I can't get financial help, at least John can help
with the children.*

"We can meet in the Perkin's Pancake parking lot," I suggested when making arrangements for the kids to spend a weekend with John. On the agreed-upon day, I sat in the car, watching customers walk into and out of the restaurant while Lizzy, Kimmy, and Chuck huddled in the back seat, reading comic books and playing word games. The sun was shining. Against the blue hue of the sky, the clouds looked like dragons. In a few minutes, John pulled into a parking spot, and I was ready to make a smooth transition. I got out of the car with the kids and gathered up their gear to make the hand-off.

John got out of the his truck, his brow furrowed, his body tense. The door slammed and—out of the blue—he turned toward me and started yelling, "You are so selfish!" His voice was loud enough to draw the attention of the customers who had the unfortunate luck of walking by at just that moment. All of a sudden, a cloud cover came out of nowhere and put us all in shadow. "You're a terrible mother," he said in easy earshot of Lizzy, Kimmy, and Chuck. "I'll take the kids and give them the good weekend they deserve, the kind of environment you refuse to give them. You're a terrible mother," he repeated, grabbing their bags and shuttling them into his truck, leaving me silent, stunned, and not a little embarrassed. I knew John's words were untrue, but his anger wrapped me in a body bag, and I couldn't get out. I wasn't sure what I had done to deserve his wrath other than exist, which seemed to remind him of his own mistakes. I drove home in a state of shock, feeling impotent to manage our family dynamics. I wanted to cry, but I didn't know where the tears were.

The cloud cover grew darker, and a few raindrops hit my windshield. *Don't you dare cry. Pull yourself together. You're better than this. Stand tall. He's right. I'm a terrible mother. I can't manage the family. I'm a failure. I'm a wimp. I just want to crawl up in a ball. I don't know what to do. You're not a terrible mother. You can do it. You have to do it. I want to die. I think I'm going to throw up.*

To supplement my income, I began to waitress at a Red Lobster on Saturday and Sunday nights, which meant I was working seven days a week. I asked John to babysit on one of those weekend nights each week. "No!" he refused as I imagined the smoke coming out of his ears over the telephone. "I'll take the kids when it's good for me and them, not when it's good for you."

"I'm not asking you to babysit so I can go on a date, John," I explained, trying to talk rationally to a hungry alligator. "I'm asking so I can work to make money so we can live." The answer was still no. Instead, my teenage daughter, Lizzy, babysat those nights and became a surrogate parent, making dinner for Kimmy and Chuckie and ensuring they got to bed at a reasonable hour. No matter how level-headed I thought I was, I seemed to run into a wall. My natural inclination was to suck things up and project calm. Internally, though, I felt trapped, like I was boxed in at every turn. How, I wondered, could I cushion this transition for my children under these conditions?

At some point after moving into our yellow-brick house, I stopped loving my children. More accurately, I loved my children deeply, but I couldn't feel that love anymore. It disappeared and I couldn't find it. Because my sense of self had become so fragile, the bonds I felt with my children became fragile too. We could be playing a game, taking a walk, or watching our favorite movie together when a chasm would open and devour me.

One Friday night, Kimmy, Chuckie and I marched into Blockbuster Video for some good weekend entertainment. It had been a busy week at school for all of us, and we were ready to let down and enjoy ourselves. Our ages and interests were all over the map, so we compromised on *The Princess Bride*, *RAD*, and *Better Off Dead*, a wonky collection reflecting our differences. After dinner, Kimmy made popcorn and we gathered around for a marathon night of film.

As the scenes radiated from the television screen, I could feel my week's worth of professional adrenaline slowly leak away. Ordinarily, that would be a good thing—it was TGIF, after all. But in its place wasn't that wholesome sense of freedom, relaxation, and settling-in-for-the-weekend-with-the-people-you-could-be-yourself-with. Instead, a host of frightening feelings and jarring questions pushed their way into my awareness.

A sense of dread. *What's happening? What's going on? Why does it feel like I'm looking at everything through a veil?* Kimmy got up to get another handful of popcorn.

A sense of panic. *Who are these kids? I know they're mine, but are they?* Chuckie rolled over on the floor three times before his eyes refocused on the TV screen.

A sense of despair. *I'm afraid. I don't belong here. I know I love them, but why can't I feel the love?* The kids were riveted by the plot and laughing quietly at the absurdity.

A sense of fear. *I feel like I'm going crazy. My whole body hurts. I'm a stranger in my own home.* "Where's Lizzy? Does anyone know where Lizzy is?"

These feelings of disorientation, fogginess, and not belonging happened more frequently as time went on. Eventually, I felt that way all the time. Home, my earth-mother domain, became a foreign country where I didn't exist in my own body and my surroundings were unreal. I would later learn these sensations are symptoms of dissociation: *depersonalization* means you feel like you are out of body and disconnected from the world, and *derealization* means your environment or sense of place feels unreal. It was the long, slow process of my *decompensation*, the psychological term for a complete mental breakdown in coping strategies. In simple terms, I felt like I wasn't me.

I'm going crazy, I thought. *It's crazy to love my children from the depths of my soul, but not feel that love. It's crazy to feel like I'm not their mother when I've always loved being their mother. It's crazy that I can't reach through this fog, I can't touch what's real, I can't feel at all.*

Soul sorrow consumed me, caused by the underground dissociative gymnastics of my mind.

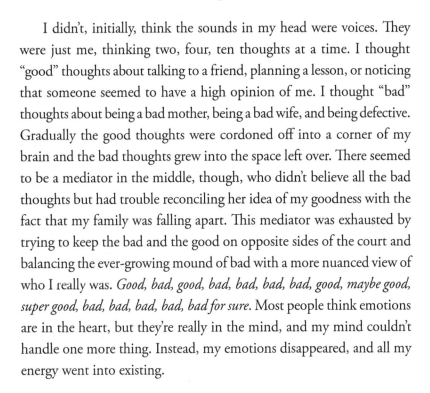

I didn't, initially, think the sounds in my head were voices. They were just me, thinking two, four, ten thoughts at a time. I thought "good" thoughts about talking to a friend, planning a lesson, or noticing that someone seemed to have a high opinion of me. I thought "bad" thoughts about being a bad mother, being a bad wife, and being defective. Gradually the good thoughts were cordoned off into a corner of my brain and the bad thoughts grew into the space left over. There seemed to be a mediator in the middle, though, who didn't believe all the bad thoughts but had trouble reconciling her idea of my goodness with the fact that my family was falling apart. This mediator was exhausted by trying to keep the bad and the good on opposite sides of the court and balancing the ever-growing mound of bad with a more nuanced view of who I really was. *Good, bad, good, bad, bad, bad, bad, good, maybe good, super good, bad, bad, bad, bad, bad for sure.* Most people think emotions are in the heart, but they're really in the mind, and my mind couldn't handle one more thing. Instead, my emotions disappeared, and all my energy went into existing.

I was not the only one experiencing soul sorrow, perhaps of a different sort. Lizzy began hanging out with older high school kids who exposed her to temptations she wasn't strong enough to resist. Before our separation, John and I had taken her to a therapist who said, "She's the angriest young lady I've ever seen." This surprised both John and me because she hadn't been expressing overt anger but had let her grades fall and had disconnected with us and our family activities. After we separated, her withdrawal turned into the rage the therapist had bookmarked. The once animated, happy little girl became an alienated, rebellious teenager. She had pulled away, at the same time John had pulled away, at the same time I had pulled away, each of us for our own reasons.

One night after our separation, Lizzy stayed out all night and slept until noon the next day. I confronted her about her behavior as she headed out again. "Lizzy, you need to let me know where you are and what you're doing. You're never around and I worry about you," I said, my whole body pleading for her cooperation. "You have homework assignments to complete. I'll help you if I can. I'm setting rules for your own good." She lunged toward the front door, zoning me out, agitated. "Listen, you can't live in this house if you don't obey the rules," I said, putting my foot down.

Lizzy grabbed the doorknob and turned around to face me, eyes flashing, her beautiful face contorted with rage. "No wonder Dad cheated on you," she spewed. "You're such a bitch!" She swirled around and stomped out of the house, leaving behind a cloud of pain. I stood there immobilized, devastated, totally blown away. I had never told the children about John's affair, and to my knowledge, he hadn't either, but bad news travels fast. Somehow, Lizzy had learned the truth. Tragically, neither John nor I had the emotional capacity to help Lizzy address her very acute needs. When she was crying out for supervision, loving attention, and a united front from her parents, we were both checked out.

Chuckie, our youngest, turned eight the year we separated. His anger was so fierce that he pounded holes in his bedroom wall and tried to jump off a porch roof. "I hate you," he screamed when I grounded him in his bedroom for some minor misdemeanor.

"You can come out when you apologize and agree to clean up the mess you made downstairs," I said, mustering up the calmest, firmest voice I could find. The slightest thing would trigger him into torrents of rage. Behind his closed door, I heard him banging away on something hidden from my view. I worried about the pounding, so I opened his door to the sight of a large gash in the wallboard, an imprint of his fist with veins spreading like tributaries to the perimeter of the molding. His window that led to the roof of our front porch was open, and he had crawled through, standing tall and threatening to jump. I sat on the floor next to the window and talked him down. He pulled himself back into his bedroom. We were both overwhelmed by the feelings too painful to feel.

A short time later, Chuckie was kicked out of his small, country private school for bad behavior. His teacher had an easygoing style which didn't match Chuckie's need for structure. I worked hard to help her set up an environment he could succeed in to no avail. The school and I mutually parted ways, and I approached the superintendent of the local public-school district to explain the situation. He found a teacher for Chuck who was kind yet structured in her approach. Chuckie flourished in that environment, was well-behaved, and finished third grade with all As.

Toward the end of the first year of our separation, I walked into Lizzy's bedroom and saw her immobilized, staring out the window. When I looked closer, I saw a sharp knife on the bed and oozing blood from her wrists staining her sheets. "Lizzy, oh, Lizzy, oh no!" I said, catching my breath. "What have you done? Are you okay?" I draped my arms around her body and pulled her toward me, looking into her eyes, watching her breathing, examining her wrists.

"I don't want to live anymore," she said in a weak voice. I helped her up, and she was able to walk. I bundled her into our car and drove her to the local hospital where she received in-patient mental health support for a month. My own emotional state was tenuous, and I barely remember the details of that family trauma, only the angst of knowing that she was hurting, and I didn't have the emotional wherewithal to help her deal with her pain. I wanted to be her mother in every sense of that word, but I couldn't. I was imprisoned in a dissociative cocoon whose silken threads were the bars on my jail cell. I was unable to be present in the moment.

My daughter, my daughter, I silently wailed for my own heart to hear. *My dear, beautiful girl. You're suffering. You're in pain.* Numbness.

What happened to make you want to take your life? I've failed you so miserably. I can't reach you. I can't reach anyone anymore. I'm so sorry. Numbness.

Tears ran rivulets down my cheek.

I love you more than life itself. If there is a God, please, please, help my daughter and all my children. Help me. Heal us. Numbness.

Help each of us, the children and John too. We're all messed up. What's happening? What's going on? Turn us into the people we're supposed be. Make us whole again. Fear. Darkness. Unbearable pain.

The shimmering icicles stood constant guard. I curled into bed, pulled the covers over my head, and detached from the world that hurt almost everywhere I turned.

While Lizzy rebelled and attempted to take her life and Chuckie got in trouble at school and pounded holes in his bedroom wall, Kimmy remained quiet, observing the drama, taking in the chaos around her. She was obedient and well mannered, a good student, and liked by everyone. She didn't cause any trouble, and it was easy to forget her in the shadows of our lives. Not that I forgot her—I always knew her beautiful young spirit was there—but she sometimes got overlooked as I ran from crisis to crisis, putting out fires. A cloud hung over her just as it hung over all of us, and I wondered: how will she escape the storm?

The years had taken a toll. Each of us was an automaton going through the motions, acting out our pain or stuffing it deep within. A fog formed a protective outer armor that enabled me to get through each day yet left me with the residue of knowing that I had no agency in my life or my children's lives. Our frozen family portrait projected a dramatically different scene from the one we projected when we first moved into the yellow-brick house. Just five years later, our smiles, our eyes, and our hearts had changed shape on the canvas, no longer formed by my dreams but rather by life forces we barely understood.

≈

In the chaotic days after my marriage fell apart, I fell in love with Peter, a man I met one weekend at a Quaker study center. Strolling between redwoods and sugar maples, skirting organic gardens, and wading through the meadow, we shared our lives and our hopes and our dreams. We wrote poetry to each other.

God is a question, an answer, searching, stretching inside, never feeling complete, melancholy, gray mist, rainy day, but not quite, sun peeking out from behind a cloud, teasing, hiding again. The words poured out of me. *Where is the glorious sunny day? Where is God?*

Peter's presence offered me breathing space from the acute pain I felt at home. His faith, self-reflection, and passion for possibilities inspired me at my depths. He was as broken as I, and our relationship was doomed to end. Yet he held me in his arms when I asked him, "How do I believe in God?"

"You yearn for it," he said simply.

So, in the silence, and with a broken heart, I began to yearn for it.

CHAPTER 4

WHAT A WIMP

As the school grew, new teachers were hired, and my class became a multi-graded first and second grade. In the fourth year of the school, the little one-room schoolhouse moved to a new building with sixty students and four teachers. I was forty-one years old, two years after John and I had separated. My students sat in a circle on the blue shag rug, talking about what kind of class pet they wanted. The year before, they had been diligent fundraisers, baking and selling cookies, running a Good Value store, and doing odd cleanup jobs around the school to earn some extra cash for our classroom kitty.

"Look, we've raised twenty-five dollars!" said one little girl as she pointed to the thermometer on the wall that kept track of our earnings. I wanted them to learn the value of hard work. When the previous year's class had wanted a pet, we began to earn and save our money. This year, half of that class had moved on, but the other half remained behind with a new crop of first graders in their stead. Because the school was still small, a pet in our room would essentially become a school pet, and the former members of the class would still be able to enjoy the joys of pet ownership.

With money in the classroom bank, it was time to decide what kind of pet we wanted. The year was 1988, a presidential election year, and George H. W. Bush and Michael Dukakis were the candidates.

Our country was in a time of big decision-making, and I wanted the children to experience a bit of what it was like to take part in a fair, democratic decision-making process.

"This year, our country will decide who our next president will be," I explained. "The candidates will make speeches and your parents will listen to what they have to say. Then all the adults in the country will go into voting booths and cast their ballots for the candidate of their choice. Their votes will be counted, and the candidate with the most votes will become president. Voting is a pretty quick process. There's a couple of months of heavy campaigning, and then it's over. There will be winners and losers, but this is democracy, and it's a fair way to make decisions.

"There's another way of making fair decisions, though," I went on. "Quakers decide important questions through consensus—lots of talking with each other, researching pros and cons, and sitting in silence, knowing that God will help us make a good choice. Quakers don't vote. They wait until everyone agrees before they move on. Essentially, consensus for Quakers means coming to agreement between you, me, and God. It takes a long time, sometimes years, but in the end, everyone is happy with the decision because everybody listens to everybody else and no one is left behind. There are no winners and losers in Quaker consensus. Everyone wins."

The kids were excited. They cared about making decisions because they had to make a lot of them every day. They also cared about fairness because they wanted to get a fair shake too. "Okay, let's try both forms of decision-making and see what we think of them. We'll decide what kind of pet to buy with our twenty-five dollars using consensus. Then we'll decide what to name our pet by voting."

"Yay! Let's do it," the class shouted, ready to get to work. Deciding on a pet through consensus required real effort. Every child spent time researching a pet of their choice, what food and shelter the pet would need, and what attention they'd require from us once they were a part of our classroom. The children each had the opportunity to bring their ideas to our group meetings and share what they had learned. Everyone asked questions and became part of the bigger conversation about what pet would be the best for our classroom. We sat in meeting for worship in silence to let God work inside us too. Six weeks later, after we had examined every pro and con for each possible pet, we decided that a parakeet would be the most fun, easy to care for, and within our price range. Everyone was on board. No one felt unheard.

The next step in the process was naming the beautiful baby-blue parakeet I bought with the money the children had raised. This decision would be made by a schoolwide election. Our timing coincided with the last week of the presidential election, so we decided we would take one week to make our decision. The kids formed three different groups, equivalent to political parties, to come up with a name. Once each group had decided on a name, they campaigned, made posters, wrote speeches, stumped through all the classrooms, and went through a lot of hoopla to convince everyone else to vote for the name they had chosen. When the big day finally arrived, we held our schoolwide election with blind ballots. We were all excited.

In the end, our parakeet was dubbed Oliver, determined by majority vote. There was singing and dancing in the streets of our school, but one little girl was unhappy. Her chosen name hadn't won. She felt like a loser. She was bummed. The class talked at length about what had happened, and we comforted those who had "lost." Both consensus and voting were fair, we agreed. Consensus took a long time to achieve, but everyone was happy. Voting was relatively quick, but some people were disappointed. There was no right or wrong, but it was good to know some of the different ways decisions could be made and the pros and cons of each.

I had fun teaching my students about consensus and voting. The children learned by experience, and they loved it. I felt competent and fulfilled, as if I were accomplishing something important. Even better, consensus filled a deep need in me. People listened to each other and affirmed each other, something I had little experience with in my nuclear and extended families.

Home is often considered the classic soft landing, the mythic place sung about in ballads and holiday tunes, yet the contrast between my home and my work was dramatic. I spun magic in my classroom, not the misery I seemed to spin at home. I had two lives: one marked by sanity and competence, the other enmeshed in craziness and chaos. *How can this be?* I wondered daily when I entered my classroom with confidence and went home to my family deflated. *How is it that these children respond so well to me when my own children respond so poorly? How is it that I feel authentic love for these kids when I seem to have lost the love I feel for my own kids? It's like I'm totally different people. The person I used to be in my family is gone. What's going on? Who am I?*

I would later learn that it's not uncommon for dissociative survivors of trauma to excel at work while they're emotionally decompensating at home. Because trauma is controlled by the *back brain*, or emotional center, using the *front brain* in charge of rational thought is an effective grounding technique. By focusing on what I could do cognitively, it took my mind off the traumatic residue incapacitating me.

I don't know what's happening in that place called home, but here, in the classroom, I am in control, I told myself. *Here, in the classroom, my love is reciprocated. Here, in the classroom, nobody will hurt me. Here, in the classroom, I am safe.*

Days wore into weeks, and weeks wore into months and years as our fragmented lives became the new normal. When my children needed me most, I was not emotionally available. The worst part was, I knew it. I wanted to be the attentive, loving, effective parent I once was, but I couldn't. Every corner of our home still palpated with pain.

After our separation, John remained in our area for about a year and then found a visiting professorship in the Southwest which took him far away from our family. On a trip back East, he spent some time backpacking with Lizzy. When they returned, he stopped at the house. "I'm taking Lizzy to live with me," he informed me. "She can attend high school at the university lab school. Because I'm a visiting professor, I have privileges that will allow for that. She wants to come with me." I felt disempowered because the decision had been made before I even knew it was a possibility. Yet I also felt relief. I was barely holding on emotionally, financially, and as a parent, and I was betting Lizzy would benefit from time away from the family drama.

"Is this what you want, Lizzy?" I asked her.

"Yeah, I think it will be pretty cool." Lizzy was a smart young girl who had lost her way in the face of our family dysfunction, and I expected this new venue would challenge her in a good way. Just a little more than a year ago, she had tried to take her life. Talking about going to school in the Southwest brought that life back into her deep-brown eyes. This seemed like a wonderful way to give her a new lens to imagine her future. I was glad she would have this opportunity. I was also glad that John would lift more of the load.

"Thank you, John," I said. "I think this will be a great opportunity for Lizzy." We contacted the local school district for permission and made plans for Lizzy to drive across country with her dad. With John and Lizzy relocated, Kimmy and Chuck were at home with me.

Lizzy's time with her dad in the Southwest was short-lived but served the purpose of getting her out of her downward spiral. She and John both returned to Pennsylvania the following year. She finished her senior year of high school locally, still uncertain of her path, and John resettled into his tenure-track position. Sometimes he took the children over the summers for opportunities I was not able to provide. When they traveled the country, they camped, visited national monuments, and made trips to Disneyland. When he was away, he stayed connected with postcards, letters, and phone calls. He loved them and they loved him. The communication between him and me, on the other hand, continued to be painful, and the time he spent with the children was always on his terms, rarely on a mutually agreed-upon schedule. His anger bumped up against my victimhood every single time.

Our divorce was finalized three years after I learned of John's affair.

The property settlement took an additional three years, carrying us well beyond the yellow-brick house. *This is all my fault,* I told myself over and over again. *The children's pain is in direct proportion to mine, and what does that mean? Look at them. Other kids come through far worse trauma than we've gone through and manage well. What have I missed on the edges of our lives that could derail them so profoundly? I've made such a mess of things.*

Stop groveling. It's not your fault. You're working hard on all fronts, and you're doing your best with very little help from John. You can't go backward; you have to go forward. I'm not sure where you're going, but I know you can get there. You can. How can I? I can barely move. My body aches. My mind is a mess. Everything I ever wanted in life—happy children and loving family—has slipped through my fingers. What irony that I've lost what I value most. And I don't seem to be able to do anything about it. I'm so confused. I don't deserve to live. I want to die. I couldn't shut the voices up.

Increasingly, the part of me who lived at home, coping with the crises of the day, seemed different from the part of me who taught school and grew in faith. Indeed, it seemed like many parts of me were passing the ball back and forth, depending on what was happening at the time. This shared power between competence and craziness should have allowed me at least a hint of sanity, but instead it served to make me feel even more crazy. The disparity between the two realities was disorienting and painful.

"I want to go to this party tonight, Mom," Kimmy begged one Saturday afternoon when she was in middle school. We were walking in opposite directions through the living room when she hit me with her plea.

I stopped mid-step and turned to look at her. "No, Kimmy, you didn't do any of your chores this week, so you've lost the privilege of going to a party. You know the rules." Teenage hormones had loosened her stuffed emotions, and they were leaking from their hiding places. She had been pushing the envelope for weeks and I was trying to set boundaries. I walked upstairs to clean the bathroom, and she followed me with a vengeance.

"I want to go, and you can't stop me," she said, standing menacingly in the doorway.

I turned to her and said, "Kimmy, you can't go." I attempted to walk past her to get away from what I perceived as threatening behavior. She followed me from room to room, making her case as her voice got louder and louder, or so it seemed to me. Internally, I was terrified. She was a sweet, sensitive girl who was testing house limits, but some part of me became confused. *What is she doing?* I whispered to myself, believing I was in mortal danger. *I'm a terrible person. I'm defective. I'm not worthy to live. Why else would she be acting this way?* The icicles began to sway, but they didn't have the capacity to protect me. I escaped into our small kitchen. She marched right behind me, her face only inches from the back of my head. The pine cabinets closed in on me and I felt trapped.

"You can't stop me," she said again. *What's happening? I don't know what's happening. All I know is I don't deserve to live. I don't want to live. I can't handle this. I might as well die. Get me out of here. Die.* I opened the utensil drawer, grabbed a knife, turned to her and said, "Here, take it. Kill me. Just kill me now," as I thrust the blade handle into her hands. She looked at me in horror, dropped the knife, and ran from the room while I crumpled and fell to the floor.

What just happened? What have I done? How could I say that to her? Why did I say that? I lay dazed and confused, then pulled myself up and found my way to my bedroom where I curled into a ball and stared into space. I didn't even have the presence of mind to check on Kimmy to make sure she was okay. While her behavior may have been unacceptable, it was still within the range of obstinate teenage anger. My behavior was beyond the pale and within no sane person's limits. I was hurting my daughter with my craziness, and I knew it.

I began journaling, mostly to set goals for myself, to make that last-ditch effort, over and over again, to gain control of my inner landscape. Take a walk. Eat healthy. Do something fun. Spend time with the kids.

If I do good things for myself, I'll stop acting crazy. If I take care of myself and live a healthy life, these bizarre feelings and behaviors will go away. My goals were never reached. A new drama always inserted itself in my life, and my good intentions were interrupted. I was grasping for sanity, and it was elusive.

One day, I was driving down my street when some thoughts and images swirled through my mind and almost stopped me in my tracks. I jerked the car to the curb, grabbed a notebook and pencil, and wrote:

> *Red*
> *Bursts forth in anguish and pain.*
> *Black creeps out to fill the cracks,*
> *Then covers all.*
> *Dead center.*
> *Dead.*

The writing left me raw. I didn't know what it meant, but I knew it was the truth. Thus began my journaling that went beyond the writing of lists of goals intended to get me back on track. This was, instead, a stream-of-conscious flow of thoughts and feelings that poured through me. Poems that were never written as poems stood out on a page of what may otherwise have been incomprehensible ramblings.

> *When the inner light goes out*
> *and the body moves along without direction,*
> *suicide relights the extinguished fire,*
> *gives meaning to the final inspiration.*

One night, I was having dinner with some other teachers at a local bar and grill. We were taking a holiday from the classroom and socializing away from our students. The dark wooden walls and candles on the tables made the setting cozy and intimate. The smell of brick-fired beef and home-brewed ale permeated the room and settled comfortably between the four of us. We chatted and laughed about the normal trivia of our lives. As the night wore on, we reluctantly gave in to the hour and paid our bill to go. On the way out the door, I passed by a mirror in the hallway and caught a glimpse of someone I didn't recognize reflected back to me. I stopped and let the other teachers go ahead as I peered into the mirror again. There was a woman. It was me. Only I was dead. It was my dead face.

I walked out the door to my car, stunned, immersed in the possibility I might be dead, and drove the short distance home in a stupor. As I settled into my house, I couldn't feel my body. I wasn't a part of my forty-year-old frame. The room around me faded in and out. I was disconnected to all feeling, emotional and physical. I wasn't real. At some point that I cannot recall, some part of me wrote in my journal:

> *Pretend I never existed.*
> *I never existed.*
> *Don't hurt me anymore.*
> *Are you there? Is someone there?*
> *Do not give me gifts.*
> *Do not cry over me.*
> *I am not here.*
> *Do not drink with me or laugh with me.*
> *I am not here. I never was.*

It was all too much. *My mind hurts. I don't belong in this world.* The children would be better off without me. *My body hurts. I can't move another step.* The world would be a better place without me. *I am useless. I am so tired of living.* I was worthless, defective, incompetent, and in unbearable pain. *I am so tired of fighting.* I finally decided to do what I knew I was meant to do. *Release me. Let me go.* I slept restlessly that night and waited until the children were out of the house the next morning before I counted out the ten remaining Wellbutrin pills in the little container with a white cap. *Take care of my children. They are precious.* I poured myself a large glass of water, wrapped myself in an old quilt, and lay on the living room sofa, taking one pill at a time. *Soon it will be over. Soon I will be done.* I closed my eyes and began drifting off. *It's all my fault. It's all my fault. It's all my—*

Good God. I don't want to die. I switched gears like a race car driver peels out his radials. As surely as I wanted to die one minute, I wanted to live the next. With a burst of energy, I pulled myself up from my prone position, ran to the telephone, and called a friend who sometimes babysat for my kids. "I've just overdosed on medication. I wanted to die. Now I don't. Help me, please." She dropped what she was doing and drove to my house to pack me off to the hospital where the toxic substance was removed from my body. The hospital released me. I went home as if nothing had happened. After all, I was a teacher, wasn't I?

Inner disagreement about my fate was only just beginning. *I'm going to live until I die!* said one voice who wanted to seize the day no matter how desperate I might feel at any given moment.

Ha, croaked another voice, *you can't even commit suicide well. You failed at that too. You're pathetic. What a wimp.*

≈

"Let's take a walk and talk," said my mentor, Paul, as we stood in the shade of the massive trees on a neatly landscaped college campus. It was a beautiful spring day, and we were at an international education symposium with other Quakers. Paul was a Quaker by birth and a professor of English at a Quaker college. I had met him at the study center when he was leading a workshop for heads of Quaker schools. He was brilliant, wise, and attentive to newbies like me who were learning the ropes.

I was in my sixth year at the school, forty-two years old, and in my third year post-separation from John. Over the past 365 days, I had achieved two milestones: I had survived a secret suicide attempt, and I had been appointed head of the Quaker school. The crazy existed in someone else's brain, so I locked it away, leaving room for excitement about my new position. I wanted to create the kind of environment for the teaching staff I had created for the students in my classroom: supportive, nurturing, challenging, educational, and fun. I found encouragement in knowing I could achieve professionally even as the rest of my personhood seemed in question.

"Paul, I want to believe in God," I said as we walked and talked, talked and walked. "I don't know how. I believe in everything that goes along with it, but I just can't cross the finish line. I don't know how to believe in God." A light breeze mixed delicately with the warm sun to glaze my cheek as other students and conference-goers strolled crisscross around the campus.

Paul listened intently, as he always did. He didn't try to fix it for me; he just tried to understand. Finally, he said, "Lyn, you don't have to believe in God to be a Quaker." Paul was referring to the *God* word. Some Quakers are uncomfortable with it and prefer to use *Light*, *Divine Being*, *Felt Presence*, or some other, less loaded word. A cloud brushed past the sun, creating a touch of shadow on the folder filled with conference paraphernalia resting lightly in my arms.

Without hesitation I pleaded, "I don't care if I'm a Quaker, Paul. I want to believe in God!"

After more walking and talking, Paul said, "It sounds like you're afraid to disappoint your father, Lyn."

"Ha! That's ridiculous. I disappoint my father all the time, Paul!" No one could ever fully satisfy my father's mercurial expectations, I mused silently with amusement. Still, Paul's words hung in the air as he left me to attend a workshop. I stayed behind and sat under a tree. The aroma of new lilac saturated the space all around and sheltered me in its grace.

I was rattled. Something inside me shifted. I couldn't move and I didn't want to.

Something's different, I experienced without words. In my heart, that little tug became a huge explosion, an earthquake moving the ground beneath me. It wasn't scary. It was liberating. *I can feel it. I was hidden behind a wall my father built, but now I'm not. The bricks of the wall are tumbling down all around me. I can feel it. Oh my. They're scattered all around. Look. The world is different when the wall is gone. It was his wall, not mine. I don't have to hide behind it. I can walk through the rubble and explore the world on my own.*

All of a sudden, I began to cry, breathing in big gulps of air and breathing out a lifetime of unknowing. *I can believe in God,* I realized, with an unexpected sense of freedom. I had been experiencing God in Quaker meeting and in my daily life over the past few years, but I hadn't had the agency to believe. *All I have to do is choose. It's my choice. It doesn't matter what my father thinks. I can believe in God if I want to.*

Back home, spring was in full bloom. I had a lilt to my step and an eagerness to talk about what had happened. When I picked up thirteen-year-old Kimmy from her piano lesson, I spilled out my story to her teacher, who was a longtime, faithful Christian. She grinned from ear to ear and exclaimed, "You were born again!"

"I guess so," I replied without enthusiasm. I hated to disappoint her, but it didn't feel like the right tagline or descriptor. In my mind, this wasn't a conversion experience. Instead, I had been trapped behind a wall not of my own making, where a small seed had taken root. Now, with the wall crumbled around that little plant, a flower unfolded in the sunlight. I had always had faith; I just couldn't access it before. On a beautiful spring morning, alone under a tree on a college campus, I received the faith I'd always had.

⌒

Dear Marriage,

There is no doubt in my mind that I felt true peace and happiness inside your walls for a very long time. Love and laughter rang from the rafters. But even as we laughed, your foundation was beginning to weaken, and I didn't see that. All was not as I thought it was. Little by little, pieces of the house began to crumble. I couldn't believe it. I wouldn't believe it. I fought it every step of the way. Sometimes I still fight it. My children were the truth tellers. They knew there was something wrong before John and I knew. They could feel the foundation rock. What was already difficult to hold together became almost impossible as they pounded on the walls in search of some kind of assurance, and the weakness of your foundation became apparent. But I never knew.

Marriage, by the time I abandoned you, I was exhausted. I was trying to hold you together when all along, John had been taking you apart, piece by piece, nail by nail. I know I took a few pieces down myself, but for every piece I may have dismantled, I nailed twenty more back in place. I tried to hold it together. I tried to stuff the cracks, but I couldn't do it by myself. You collapsed right under me. Marriage, it hurts me to have to bury you. The pain of losing you is very deep. But you are no more. I want to lay your pieces to rest.

Lyn

PART 2

Real or Make-Believe?

1991–2001

Real or Make-Believe?

It is raining outside. I can hear it. Inside, it is not raining.
Instead, there is a dull, heavy fog that lies thick across my forehead.
It clouds my mind and keeps me from knowing myself.
I have to function. I wonder if I'm real.
I believe that all of my multiple personalities are made up—
make believe.
So, logically, then, I must be make-believe. I am just a figment of my
own imagination.
So, when I get too tired, I can just crawl into a hole and disappear.
But my real children are not make-believe.
And their pain is real.

April 1993

CHAPTER 5

THE NUTCRACKER SUITE

Two years after my failed suicide attempt, my friend Thelma and I sat around my kitchen table, plotting my escape from the craziness that had taken up residence in my mind. The sun shone through the tiny window, illuminating the same pine cabinets that had closed in on me several years before. As I vacillated between unremitting pain and the compunction to take control, I remembered begging my daughter to kill me in that very room. I was horrified by the reality of my internal chaos. The solution, I decided, was to confine myself to the safety of a psychiatric hospital.

I was forty-three years old. After working with two different therapists, daily journaling, frequent goal setting, medications out the wazoo, and trying just about anything under the sun, I was not better. I was worse. My thinking and emotions didn't match. I was fragile, frightened, and my body felt like a truck was rolling over it. I was a spectator sitting on a perch in the corner of a room, out of body, watching this wretched woman go through the motions of life, unable to function in spite of the fact that in my professional life I was functioning, and highly effectively at that. So, I made the decision to check myself into the women's unit of Northwestern Institute, a psychiatric hospital an hour away.

Thelma had a commanding presence and had befriended me at Quaker meeting. She shepherded me through my angst. She gave me advice. She offered help. "You will NOT drive yourself to the women's unit," she insisted. "You think you're invulnerable, but you need support. I'll go with you." At that moment, I didn't feel invulnerable, but admitting that wasn't my strong suit, so I acquiesced.

"Sure. I'd like you to drive me."

Through a fog of pain and uncertainty, I went through the motions of checking with hospital admissions for bed availability. I gave the woman on the telephone my insurance information to make sure I was covered. *I don't have any choice, do I? If I can't take care of myself, then maybe someone else will take care of me.* Hospitalization seemed the only route.

Thelma, on the other hand, was strong and confident. She was a public-school teacher ten years my senior. Her gentle yet firm approach to kindergarten children had won her awards and were the same qualities that made me feel safe around her. It was as if some unseen thread had pulled us together, she my mentor, I the student.

"Children have the inner capacity to navigate and make sense of their worlds," Thelma would declare when we veered onto educational topics. "They learn by doing and, for young children, that means play. If we give them the opportunity, their play teaches them what they need to know and prepares them for the next steps in their learning." Thelma was a very creative kindergarten teacher.

"Sitting in desks is BORING!" she added.

"Yes," I agreed enthusiastically. The teacher in me was always inspired by Thelma, and I added my own experiences of active, child-centered classrooms to our conversations. Our relationship was professionally stimulating and personally reassuring.

Yet deeper still was another connection we couldn't have known when we met. Thelma had been diagnosed with a dissociative disorder and had been working with a therapist to heal from the trauma of early childhood sexual abuse. She appeared to be more centered in her life than I was in mine, in spite of the fact that her challenges seemed more daunting. She was in control of her life, and I was most definitely not in control of mine. On her way out my front door, she turned and looked directly into my eyes as she prepared me for what lay ahead.

"Go to the hospital," she said. "Get help. You can't do it alone."

I lay down on my big double bed, alone, listening to the sounds of silence pushing up against my skull. In the distance, I heard the television playing a *Ponderosa* rerun and imagined Kimmy and Chuck were watching it somewhere, but I didn't know for sure, and I was too spaced out to care. How odd. I used to care so much that we took the television out for a year so our kids could grow up interacting with each other and using their minds for creative play. Now, I just closed my eyes and felt the pulse of blood course through my veins as if my flesh were allergic to air. Sometimes it was easier not to think because when I thought, I got confused with the jumble of strands that poured through me. Where was I? Who was I? Why was I crazy, and why did I know I was crazy? Wasn't that the definition of crazy, that you were oblivious to your insanity? Oh, for the luxury of oblivion.

The plans for hospital admissions were complete. I had submitted my resignation as head of school months before, knowing my emotional state would not allow me to continue the stress of school leadership. Now, with the hospital on the horizon, I arranged for my parents to take care of Lizzy, Kimmy, and Chuck.

"I'll pick you up at eight o'clock," said Thelma over the phone. I held the receiver in the crook of my shoulder as I walked from room to room, trying to get my affairs in order while I talked. *The clothes go in this bag, the toiletries in that, the checklist is here, and phone numbers are there.* Doom hung over me as I imagined every word I said and act I took were my dying wishes, the last will and testament of the crazy woman I had become.

"An early start should give us plenty of time to get you to your admissions at nine o'clock. We might run into morning traffic and, even if we don't, it's better to get there sooner rather than later."

Ready or not, I was taking the big dive into the institutional unknown. I believed any mix of medication and medical professionals could take better care of me than I could myself.

I watched the spring buds on the trees in my small town pass by me like a kaleidoscope changing patterns as we drove the forty minutes to our destination. On the way, we talked about the events of the past few weeks that led me to this decision. It had been a warm Saturday morning several weeks prior. I stumbled out of my house into my backyard, journal in hand, while Lizzy practiced guitar, Chuckie climbed the red maple tree, and Kimmy was across the street at a friend's house. Ordinarily, I loved the outdoors; it renewed me and gave me a sense of peace. On this day, however, I was in great pain. I decided to write a letter to my therapist, Jana, who I'd been seeing for about six months on Thelma's recommendation. I wanted to tell her that I deserved to die. And I was going to make it happen. Again. I hadn't succeeded the first time I tried, but this time, I would. With my three children around me, doing the ordinary things they ordinarily did, I wrote her a letter and told her I was going to kill myself. Handwritten on both sides of eight pages of old-fashioned stationary, all of me rambled through the unexplored highways and byways of my psyche.

Dear Jana, I began, *The reason why I shouldn't live is because I don't care about my children.* This statement reflected my emotional numbness, my depersonalization and derealization, so I clarified, *I do love Lizzy, Kimmy, and Chuck very very very very much. I am truly sorry for the pain I have caused them and will cause them. I don't know why. I haven't been able to change it.* Using different handwritings that ultimately deteriorated into scribbles, I built a compelling case for my unworthiness to live, my insanity, my utter inability to manage the normal ups and downs of life. I would learn later that different handwritings are one mark of different parts of the self, but I didn't know that at the time.

Maybe you don't like me now that you know what a spoiled brat, what a wimpy shitty weakhearted cowardly incompetent thing I am, I went on, trying to justify what I perceived as my therapist's dislike of me. *Well, you may be right, but that's what I am. That's all I am. I don't want to be that anymore but I am. I want to know why. What's wrong with me? I've tried hard for four years and I've tried to keep my spirits up. But that's a lie. I am DEPRESSED. Medicine doesn't help, you don't help, the lawyers don't help, getting tough doesn't help, getting cheerful doesn't help.* Prozac, Wellbutrin, and Lithium did nothing to address my craziness, nor did my lawyer, who was negotiating my property settlement, nor my intentional attempts at being more assertive or upbeat.

I don't believe that my living is better for my kids than my dying. Sure, it would be better if I were normal. But this way, no. I'm just not good enough to live. I'm not I'm not I'm not I'm not I'm not. No No No No No No No No No No No help because there is no help. Look at this letter. What a wimp. I'm not worthy to live.

Page after page, different voices emerged out of the ink on the stationary, each with different capacities to face the future. On page six I deteriorated into scratch marks across the paper. By page twelve, I had pulled myself back together, chose a different color paper, and in very neat handwriting approached my situation rationally. *I would like to be able to have the energy just to keep going with my life and do the best I can with my kids. But this craziness is sapping so much of my energy. I watch situations and opportunities go by where I could affirm my life, in spite of the hard stuff going on. That is the role model my kids need to see, but I can't do it because this chaos immobilizes me.*

The sun was shining, but the air was still. The voices of my children were a distant din. I put my pen down, sealed the envelope, and sent the letter off to Jana.

❦

Thelma parked the car, and we walked through the large suburban campus toward the two-story building, which was well kept and clean.

I noticed immediately there were no flowers on the grounds. *I wonder why they don't have landscapers to make this a pretty place,* I said to myself. Judging from the people we saw walking into and out of the facility, it looked like a cross between a hospital and a school for down-and-outers—alcoholics and addicts, people who had been on the streets, people who were mentally ill. *I know I don't look like a lot of them, but I sure feel like they look.*

"I think this is going to be the perfect place for me," I said candidly to Thelma. What a relief to be with other people who felt like I did: sad, scared, confused, and in pain, with no idea how to cope with the next five minutes, let alone the next five years. "I'm going to fit in fine." Thelma and I hugged goodbye, and a woman took me upstairs to my room where I sat on my bed, frightened, hopeful, overwhelmed, and relieved. Somewhere in this looming tangle of bricks, mortar, people, and pain, I was certain to find a new beginning.

The women's unit was an experimental program meant to address the unique needs of women who were having difficulty coping with their lives. Rather than assuming there was something wrong with the women who were there, they operated under the premise that something, or many things, had happened to put them in the vulnerable positions they were in. They assumed the women had the capacity to cope with life if they had support, education, appropriate medication, and psychological interventions. Working out of a health model rather than a medical model, they used the time they had with clients to provide individual therapy, group sessions, twelve-step lectures, art and music therapy, family interventions, spiritual support, decision-making workshops, social work, and more.

⁔

"My name is Susan," said my roommate when I walked into my room for the first time. She was a demure woman about my age. I later learned she had been forced to give up her infant daughter when she was a teenager. Her parents had arranged for the adoption through the church without much input from Susan. Now, in midlife, she suffered from crippling depression and repressed mourning. She looked like a nice person, someone who might be safe, not someone who would hurt me. Her eyes lowered when she introduced herself, but then she forced a smile. Susan had been admitted just an hour earlier, so we walked together down the whitewashed hallway to our first daily community meeting with all the other women, on edge and glad we had each other for support.

The social worker who led the meetings was named Kelly. She often came just a little bit late—on purpose I suspected, to give us time for unsupervised interaction. A street-smart-looking lady in her late twenties sat across from me. Her name was Debbie, and her bright-red lipstick matched her curly, sexy, brown hair. She was a recovering alcoholic who chewed gum and made wisecracks, relaxed and laughing. I was afraid of her devil-may-care attitude at first, which didn't fit well with my cross-all-the-t's and dot-all-the-i's personality. "Watz up?" She threw me the ball with a grin. Behind her alcoholic bravado, I would learn, she harbored abuse by her father and confessed she sometimes abused her stepson too.

Then there was Candida, a nun who had been sexually abused by a cousin. She played the guitar and wrote a song to her perpetrator as part of her healing. A week into my stay, Candida told me, "I may not pray here in the same way I pray when I'm in the convent. But this entire experience, everything we do here, is prayer. We are praying when we share the deepest parts of our souls with our therapists or each other. We are praying when we're writing in our journals or listening to a lecture. We are praying when we're in art therapy or in the lunchroom. It's all prayer." I never forgot her words, and since then, I've discovered prayer in every moment of my day. All because Sr. Candida told me that my stay in a mental hospital was really prayer.

At that particular community meeting, the social worker asked us to check in with how we were feeling. Karen had two illegitimate children and was knocked around by her boyfriend daily while her mother took drugs and her father was in jail. She paced the floor while she talked, confused and unsure of her next steps. Margo was a drug addict who was in recovery but struggling with self-esteem issues. She sank into the only cushy chair in the room, picking at her fingernails while she took herself apart, bit by bit. Tara looked like she should have been in high school. She had run away from an abusive home and was curled up in her not-so-comfortable straight chair, refusing to say a word. Like Tara, not everyone talked, but those who did grazed along the bottom of the well that hadn't seen water in years.

Day after day, we talked, shared our stories, lamented our predicaments, looked for answers, liked each other, didn't like each other, didn't know what to think of each other, but figured out slowly how to walk together through the pain that consumed us. Dancing into and out of each other's lives, we spun around the hallways metaphorically, pulling each other down, lifting each other up, and making space for the unexpected dance moves that revealed what we didn't know ourselves. Plie. Arabesque. Assemble. Penché. We were the *Nutcracker Suite*. That's what I called us. The people whose tears sculpted a dance of womanhood between unlikely sisters.

While my emotional state was in shambles at home, everything changed once I was admitted to the women's unit. The multiple voices that had stalked me were quiet. I was a different person here, the one I thought I knew, the one who used her mind to navigate her world. I was safe in the cloistered space. No one was going to hurt me. People listened to me and didn't think I was crazy. The lectures fed my mind and my soul. They made head sense and heart sense. While my world at home made no sense, the world in the women's unit satisfied my need for clarity, organization, and order. I quickly settled in and gobbled up the smorgasbord of therapeutic options to fill my hunger.

Susan and I shared growing-up stories. Candida and I prayed together. Debbie taught me how to paint my fingernails, something I had never, ever done before. I took it upon myself to tenderly plant and tend to flowers around the trees on the grounds that the landscapers had ignored. My crisis receded into the background. My family was no longer weighing me down. I found joy in sharing my life with other women, and they seemed happy to share their lives with me. I was stable enough to begin to work on the issues that had brought me there.

Managing destructive family dynamics was a major focus, though not a very successful one. My psychiatrist, Dr. Lance, tried to arrange a family meeting with John, who was now living less than an hour away, but he refused to participate in any way.

"I'm sorry, Lyn. We tried to contact John for a family meeting. We left several messages. When we finally got him on the phone, he said no. 'Absolutely not.'" While this was a stumbling block in creating a more workable life post-hospital, it was also information regarding what I could count on and what was a pipe dream. The professional staff was stunned that he had no interest in talking through issues that were affecting not only me but also our children and, presumably, him. I had been excusing John for years, assuming I had brought this disaster on myself. The failed effort to draw him into a rational and compassionate conversation finally convinced me that I didn't bear all the blame.

One afternoon, Dr. Lance called me into a private session. Kelly was there too. "Lyn, I've received a letter from your father," she began. I wondered why he might be writing to my psychiatrist and was optimistic it was supportive. She gave the letter to me so I could read it. Slowly, my eyes went down the page, drinking in the words he had written.

"I have a poor opinion of shrinks but feel it is my duty to write to you in spite of that fact. I expect you will honor professional ethics and keep this confidential. DO NOT SHARE THIS LETTER WITH MY DAUGHTER." That Dr. Lance's first act upon receiving the letter was to hand it over seemed positively rebellious to me. I was grateful. *Here's someone who doesn't obey my father. Hmmm. Wow. I've never known anyone who didn't obey him.*

I continued down the page, painfully aware he was writing about me. "My daughter is a bright woman. Giving credit where it is due, she inherited her genes from me. Unfortunately, she is displaying weak-minded characteristics due to the breakup of her marriage. Clearly, impugning any other reasons for her mental incapacity would be counterproductive. Do not try to pull deep, dark secrets from her, as shrinks have a tendency to do. I assure you that line of thinking has no bearing on her nervous breakdown." I was confused. *My father loves me. Maybe this is what love looks like. I love him. What does this mean? Is it normal for him to write a letter like this?* I must have spilled some of these thoughts into audible words because Kelly responded.

"No, Lyn, this is not what love looks like." Dr. Lance encouraged me to talk about how I was feeling, but I really wasn't feeling anything. Shimmering all over my body, the icicles shielded me from emotion. I was looking for sense in the letter and trying to find slivers of truth that would connect the dots. It didn't sound quite right, but it had to be true because he was my father. Like a fish who doesn't know she's swimming in water because it's all she knows, I didn't know I was peering into my family's underbelly because it was all I knew.

I had no memory of past abuse. I would sit in community meeting, listen to the horrific stories of the women around me, and realize my symptoms—my responses to situations—were the same as theirs. We all had anxiety. We all had depression. We all had fear, inner chaos, lack of self-esteem, and confusion. Many of us felt invalidated, unreal, and unworthy. Everyone could name their abusers and tell stories of their abuse. Except me.

"You have every sign and symptom," someone said, piquing my curiosity but adding form to my resistance. The gap between my inner chaos and my successful professional life—between my emotions and my mind—added fuel to the fire of my confusion. No one told me to look for memories of abuse, but I wasn't stupid. I looked around and compared myself with my unit mates. I read books that helped me understand how people respond to trauma. I noticed how my belly clenched and my heart beat faster when someone else told a terrible story. I felt the rawness that penetrated every pore of my body, and then some. I felt the tears dribble down my cheeks at the most inopportune moments. I couldn't imagine who had hurt me, but I knew someone had. If only I could find the memories, I would also find an explanation for my craziness.

Toward the end of my month in the women's unit, a friend checked the answering machine on my home phone and called to tell me the principal of an elementary school in a neighboring school district had left a message.

From the isolated pay phone in the middle of the floor of the women's unit, I spoke into the phone receiver. "Yes, this is Lyn Robertson. Thank you for leaving a message."

"Ms. Robertson, I've received your application for a first-grade teaching position and would be happy to interview you next week. Are you interested and would you be available?" As luck would have it, I was scheduled to be discharged the following week.

"Yes! Thank you," I replied, and we set up an interview appointment as I wondered what she'd think if she knew where I was calling from.

As per insurance requirements, I left the women's unit exactly thirty days after I'd entered it, vulnerable and unsure, but infinitely more stable than I had been when I entered. I was excited but nervous to leave the safety of the hospital, with all the possibility and peril that might entail. It takes twice as long to readjust to the outside as you spend on the inside, or so they say. June was behind me, and July was just around the corner. I had the rest of the summer to find my way in the real world.

And I had a job interview.

CHAPTER 6

ROSIE

My yellow-brick house was quiet when Thelma dropped me off. She had picked me up at the hospital, taken me to lunch, then helped me out of her car with my bags in hand. We hugged at the doorstep, and she left, trusting me to my own devices. "You take care of yourself," she said on her way down the sidewalk. "Call me if you need anything."

I walked through my front door. It was silent and I was completely alone. No kids running through the house. No arguments to knock me off kilter. No angry phone calls from John. Just me, myself, and I—all of us scared but hopeful. The kids would arrive the next day, but for now, solitude was my sanctuary. I could hear a pin drop.

The women's unit had helped me achieve some level of stability, but I was terrified I would backslide. The witches brew that had sent me there—a mixture of numbness and chaos—had receded while in the safe environment, giving me a false sense of control. I was sure the illusion would dissipate once I reentered the world. Yet the hospital work gave my inner world the courage to feel some real feelings. Like the outer skin of an onion peeling off the juicy, raw center, the numbness slipped off my body, revealing my raw core. All of me felt like an open wound as if I were a burn victim. On some days, a general throbbing in every pore of my body would force me to climb into my bed in the middle of the day and revert to a fetal position, unable to cope with even the slightest expectation. On other days, a balm of healing oozed over my persistent wounds. I clung to those moments of health.

My job interview had gone well. I was forty-four years old when I was hired to teach in Bethlehem, the Christmas City, a half hour away, so I decided to leave our yellow-brick house and move closer to my new employment. This compelled me to reach inside to summon up a part who could take control, make trips to my new classroom, and prepare for the children who would be arriving soon. Back and forth on my inner playing field, I threw the football from one part of me who was optimistic and capable to another part of me who was overwhelmed and consumed with pain. Like siblings guarding their turf, these parts argued with each other constantly.

I am a victim, I said to myself. *I don't care what anyone says. I am. I can't do it. I can't cope. I want someone to take care of me. I'm sick. And I'm tired. I can't do it. I feel like scum.* Another part of me argued, *No, you're not a victim. Stop acting like one. Get up and go.* Still another countered, *You are good and precious. You are taken care of. I will take care of you. Don't cry. Don't hurt.* And another, *I think I'm going crazy.* And another, *No, you're not. You're not crazy.* Out of a dark lagoon came a voice describing my visceral experience. *There is a reason. Big hole, big opening, opens, closes, opens closes. Sucks me in, spits me out.*

My small but emerging sense of power that was birthed at the women's unit prompted me to raise the stakes of the game. Lizzy, at the time, was living with friends as she prepared to go to college, so I asked John to take both Kimmy and Chuck to live with him. At the ages of fifteen and twelve, Kimmy and Chuck needed consistent parenting, and I was afraid I might not be able to give that to them. I knew I had to focus on my recovery, to discover whatever needed to be discovered, and heal it. If John really thought I was such a bad parent, now was the time to put his money where his mouth was.

"No, I'm not willing to take both of the children," John said. "Why should I? We should parent equally," he said, forgetting that for five years I had parented almost totally alone. "I'll take Kimmy and you take Chuck." I tried to explain that I needed time and space to continue the healing I had begun, but he seemed to have no sympathy. By this time, I was used to his oppositional stance and sensed arguing would get me nowhere. So, I told Chuck to pack his bags and plan on an adventure with Mom.

I journaled daily, post-hospital. Different aspects of my being took on names on the pages of the loose leaf binder. "Survivor" managed to hang in there no matter what was happening in my life. This genderless part of me acted normal and never revealed the turmoil going on inside of me. Still, Survivor was often foiled by "Victim," who would sabotage me at every turn. Victim felt like a little child, beaten into submission and abused into powerlessness. I saw their impact on me and their struggles with each other in my writing. It was disconcerting to have names for thoughts in my head, but the names seemed to magnify my feelings. Sometimes I felt like a Victim, oppressed and disabled, and sometimes I felt like a Survivor, ready to manage regardless.

I woke up one August morning, excited school would be starting soon and anxious to get my classroom in order. I dressed quickly, grabbed my teaching tools, and ran off to arrange the desks and bulletin boards. *I can do this*, thought Survivor as I drove to the school. *I am smart and strong and bright. If I can get up and get going each morning, I'll be fine.* Later in the day, at home, surrounded by the remnants of my defeated family, my voices deflated. *No, I can't*, whispered Victim. *I can barely move. It's more than I can bear*. A weight of oppression devoured me.

Nonetheless, I moved the entire contents of our house in a small town to an apartment in Bethlehem on a street with towering maples and oaks. The first floor of an old house with a big backyard was just waiting for the petunias and impatiens I would plant with care. Chuck could walk to school and throw around the baseball with new friends, and I could walk to the center of town to window-shop for books, candles, and elegant dresses I couldn't afford. We would begin this new life together and—somewhere, somehow—I was going to get better.

"Writing affirmations is a good way to get rid of the old tapes you've been told all your life," Kelly had explained during one of our community meetings in the women's unit. She taught us how to write affirmations that would eventually erase the memory links of invalidation. If you've always been told you're stupid, you have to unwind that tape. Or if you've been told you're good for nothing, or untrustworthy, or only good for sex, then you're going to go through life thinking you're stupid, good for nothing, untrustworthy, and good only for sex. "The truth is," Kelly told us, "that you're none of those things. You're smart, you have a purpose, and you are capable of being trustworthy. And although sex is a gift for adults, it's meant to be loving and consensual. You are good for sex in that context, and so much more."

Sometimes, Kelly told us, we could write our affirmations in the first person to claim our positive identity. "I am good." Sometimes, we could write it in the second person to hear someone tell us directly, "You are good." And sometimes we could write it in the third person to hear other people affirm us even if we're not around to hear it. "She is good." This worked pretty well for a person with multiple voices. Because the old tape is pretty powerful, she suggested we write the affirmation and then let the old tape challenge us to start a dialogue. She had faith that the healthy parts of us would win in the long run. In fact, sometimes our growing healthy parts might emerge to become an important part of the conversation.

I began my affirmations in the hospital and continued them over the summer and throughout the year after my discharge. In the few moments I had to myself between teaching, planning, and therapy, I would settle into my bed, turn up the volume on my radio, and churn out the words I needed to hear: "I, Lyn, am okay. I am healthy and strong." The music blared in the background, drowning out the static so I could hear the affirmative words.

Excerpts from Pages and Pages of Daily Affirmations

I, Lyn, am okay. I am healthy and strong.	I feel very shaky.
I, Lyn, am okay. I am healthy and strong.	I know I'm still sick. I'm screwed up.
I, Lyn, am okay. I am healthy and strong.	Everyone is sick. Not just me.
I, Lyn, am okay. I am healthy and strong.	It's okay to be a little crazy.
I, Lyn, am okay. I am healthy and strong.	At least I know I'm sick. And I'm working on getting better.
You, Lyn, are okay. You are healthy and strong.	You are defective. You don't know what you're talking about.
You, Lyn, are okay. You are healthy and strong.	You use and manipulate people. You try to control people.
You, Lyn, are okay. You are healthy and strong.	We don't know what to do with you. Nobody gets along with you.
You, Lyn, are okay. You are healthy and strong.	Where are you, Lyn? We need you.
You, Lyn, are okay. You are healthy and strong.	You're just not nice anymore.
She, Lyn, is okay. She is healthy and strong.	She looks tired.
She, Lyn, is okay. She is healthy and strong.	She's wearing down.

She, Lyn, is okay. She is healthy and strong.	I don't understand her.
She, Lyn, is okay. She is healthy and strong.	She doesn't know what she's doing.
She, Lyn, is okay. She is healthy and strong.	She should know what she's doing.
I, Lyn, am okay. I am healthy and strong.	Kick ass.
I, Lyn, am okay. I am healthy and strong.	Assholes.
I, Lyn, am okay. I am healthy and strong.	Men suck.
I, Lyn, am okay. I am healthy and strong.	You can't beat me.
I, Lyn, am okay. I am healthy and strong.	The fucking basement can't hurt me. And you can't either.

Thelma and I remained close over the summer the way two people do when they've shared an intimate experience. I would talk of my time in the women's unit, and she would talk of her own therapy and the places it took her. She had been diagnosed with what was then called *multiple personality disorder*, now named *dissociative identity disorder* in the *Diagnostic and Statistical Manual of Mental Disorders* (DSM).

"I'm *co-conscious*," she explained with authoritative clarity. "That means that my core personality is always present, watching, or looking in on what my 'insiders' are saying or doing. It's crazy making. I have to protect the little ones who are afraid and slow down the ones who are angry."

Dissociation, I would learn in time, is a common brain response to boredom, repetitive activity, and trauma—three totally different activities with different impacts. Almost everyone has had at least one dissociative experience in his or her life. At the light end of the scale, spacing out and becoming forgetful during stressful times may be dissociation. Midscale, looking down from the corner of the room in grief while watching a loved one slip away is dissociation. At the extreme end of the scale, dissociation may repeat itself over and over again in order to protect the child from chronic trauma. In these situations, it becomes protective in the moment but dysfunctional in the adult who is no longer in danger. Dissociative identity disorder is the most extreme form of dissociation where the child, whose personality structure is not yet fully formed, creates parts to hold the abuse so the rest of the child is unaware of the ongoing trauma and can function in the real world.

Thelma's parts were different from the nontraumatic parts of selves that everyone feels occasionally—the part that is sociable, the part that wants to stay home, the part that is ready to conquer the world. The dissociative parts that lived inside her had been sheltered by amnesic barriers to hide from herself and everyone else the trauma she had experienced. She was in the process of going back in time to her abuse experiences and having *abreactions*, or emotional release from reliving the trauma, as a part of her healing. Her diagnosis was intriguing and controversial.

Early one morning, I lay in bed, not awake but not soundly asleep. I had what some call a twilight dream that brought me to consciousness.

> *You have a twin sister,*
> *but they gave her away,*
> *and she is me,*
> *and her name is Rosie.*

Really? What does that mean? I was not prone to dreaming, but this revelation felt much like the poems that sometimes tumbled out into my journal. It made no sense, but it felt real.

I wrote the dream down because it seemed like an important message. Then I tucked it away for another day. The nursery rhyme I used to say as a little girl came to mind:

> *Ring around the rosies.*
> *Pocket full of posies.*
> *Ashes, ashes,*
> *We all fall down!*

I remembered playing this game at Vacation Bible School when I was very little. It was fun. I was safe. I felt some mysterious connection with this rhyme. Was it related to my twilight dream? I didn't know, but I was left with a riddle of my own about a twin sister I didn't have.

> *You have a twin sister,*
> *but they gave her away,*
> *and she is me,*
> *and her name is Rosie.*

I loved my parents. They were quirky, but they were all I knew. My mother was soft and loving, and she let my father walk all over her. My father, on the other hand, was hard and gruff and walked all over anyone who got in his way. He was a my-way-or-the-highway kind of guy and made lots of enemies by getting involved in local politics and writing monthly pamphlets on controversial topics that we delivered into mailboxes. People in our small, blue-collar neighborhood had a choice: they could either respect him, hate him, or fear him. He was, for all intents and purposes, a force to be reckoned with.

Not surprisingly, my parents' relationship was highly conflicted. My father yelled at my mother a lot and put her down continually. She fought back but always gave in. Even as a small child, I could never understand why she let him demean her. As much as I loved him, I hated him for hurting my mother. I wanted to protect her from his raging rants.

Still, when push came to shove, they were a unit. He may have been verbally and emotionally abusive to her, but he was her man. Many years later, after he had died and she had dementia, she told me over and over again that he was "a good man" and she "had a good life."

I visited my parents in July about three weeks after I was discharged from the women's unit to celebrate my birthday and my father's birthday. My mother made a large cake and decorated it with sweet flowers everywhere. As usual, her creations were a work of art.

"How are the children, Popup?" my father asked as he took a bite of cake. Popup was the name he had given me as a little baby when I used to pop up my head in my bassinet.

"They're doing as well as can be expected," I replied. "I'm worried about Lizzy. She's so moody and I really don't have the energy to cope with her shenanigans. I have to keep working on my healing and that takes a lot of time." We were on the back porch, looking down on the neighborhood kids playing in the alley. It was a warm day, and I noticed sweat dripping down my mother's forehead. My father drank from his coffee cup, coughed, and looked away. I didn't tell him I had a copy of the letter he had written to my shrink.

"Based on my symptoms, the professional staff at the hospital think I may have been abused as a small child," I went on. "Is there anyone you know who might have hurt me?" I hoped they would help me on this journey. "All my symptoms seem to match women who were abused as children. I don't remember any abuse, but they say that people often repress or dissociate memories. What can you tell me about my childhood that I might not remember?"

My sincere questions were met with shock. The easygoing atmosphere turned tense. My father cursed, got up from his chair, and walked off the porch, leaving his coffee cup behind. My mother began to pick up dirty plates. I pursued the only thread I had. "Could it have been Grandpa, Daddy's dad, who hurt me?" I asked, rising to help her clean up birthday remnants. "I barely remember him even though he lived with us. Everyone tells me he was cruel." Both she and my sister had used this word to describe him, so I knew my characterization was not a surprise to her. We walked into the house with our arms loaded with celebration scraps.

"Oh, no! It couldn't have been him!" My mother gave no explanation as to why it couldn't have been my grandfather. By this time, we were in the kitchen, separating plates to be washed from trash to be thrown. "It must have been that boy who lived down the alley."

My grandfather was a blip in my past, and I didn't remember any boy down the alley. I left the conversation unsettled. Maybe I had never been abused and my questions were all a wild goose chase, but I was surprised at the reaction I had received from both my parents. Rather than expressing concern and care, they were defensive and angry. If I had expected them to wrap me in parental love, they were clear I had crossed a red line. I wanted their support as my mental state was still precarious, and I was disappointed I wasn't going to get it. But I walked away without emotion. Instead, my mind observed my parents and examined the mental maze I found myself in. I wondered which twists I might take safely and which turns might lead me somewhere dark where I didn't want to go. I didn't feel anything. Like the fish in the water, I didn't know anything else.

As a teenager, I would often come home from school and sit at the kitchen table, talking to my mother. Her long black hair was pulled back in a bun, the color intact without dye until her death at the age of ninety, a badge she wore with pride. A one-time beauty, her soft, olive-colored skin had given way to a hard life that my icicled mind knew nothing about. A creative person, she had written poetry in her youth and developed her considerable talent as an artist in midlife to cope with her ongoing depression. She was interested in people and why they acted the way they acted. She listened to radio talk shows that had guests with expertise in one mental affliction or another. Then she would try to apply these theories to our family, to me, my sister, my brother, occasionally to herself, but never to my father.

"I don't think a boy will ever like me, Mom. I'm too shy," I said one day. "I don't know what to say to them. My lips tremble. I get so embarrassed. It's humiliating. For some reason, I'm afraid of boys." Trembling lips was an awful response to the kind of playful tête-à-tête my high school peers engaged in. My brain froze when a nice boy tried to talk to me, so I usually tried to avoid social interaction that might lead, one day, to dating. "I really don't know what to do," I said in despair.

"You're virginal, Lyn," my mother responded, never passing up an opportunity to analyze an interpersonal situation. "You look pure. That's why boys don't seek you out, because they're afraid of you. You're virginal." I knew what a virgin was, but I wasn't quite sure what virginal meant. I liked the sound of pure. I thought my mom was giving me a compliment or, at least, a rationalization about why I was dateless, flirtless, and friendless. Unlike my father, who was touchless, I could hug my mother and she would hug me back. We embraced and I soaked up the feeling of her soft skin. Then I went into my bedroom to do my homework.

≈

Back home, I was still spending an inordinate amount of time in therapeutic aftercare, at the same time preparing for a new life in a new city with a new job. I wrote my parents a letter.

Dear Mom and Dad, I began. *I am working hard at the things I need to do and trying to keep up my strength. Most of the time I am exhausted, sometimes I get discouraged, but at least I have a better sense of the process I am going through. That makes me feel less despair and more hopeful. Life is a journey.*

My new job helps to ground me, I continued. I described my preparations for school, my positive interactions with the teachers in the building, and the respectful way the principal treated me as a peer, which challenged my underlying fear that I was a fake. Then I told them about my aftercare. *Monday I go to family therapy with the kids, Tuesday I go to the 12-step lecture, Wednesday I see Jana, Thursday I attend a group therapy session with Jana, and Friday I attend an aftercare group therapy at the hospital. Sometimes I feel like I'm still hanging on by a thread, but I am building a strong support group of people who can help me out when I'm in crisis.*

Love, Lyn, I closed.

My father responded with a two-page typed letter. "This is probably the most difficult letter I have ever attempted," he began. He went into a full-throated attack on "psychiatry" saying, "I see my little girl sinking into a desperate no-win situation. I see the utter failure of psychiatric treatment . . . you are being led down into the valley of strange hobgoblins by quacks who should leave the practice of psychiatry to more objective and competent professionals." He made a convoluted case for the fact that all my problems had to do with my relationship with my ex-husband John.

"It is a fact your mental state is not improving. <u>Whatever relief you receive from the shrink has been fleeting</u>. You must face this fact. <u>You are not improving</u> [underlines his]." My father's passionate diatribe scorned the inner work that comes with healing and promoted, instead, his own theory. "It works only if in one's relations with others one can disabuse oneself of all 'psychiatric' imprinting, preconceived conclusions, bias, prejudices and as nearly as possible achieve the outlook . . . of the innocence of a young child(?) [question mark his]." He continued to harp back to my relationship with my husband as being the sole cause of my woes, as if any other possible cause would be an affront to him. He said my "psychiatric work" was "as spurious as a three-dollar bill."

Even I, confused woman that I was, could see there was something underneath the venom my father spewed at my course of treatment, couched as it was in parental concern. "Leave the past behind. Be a good girl. Oh, and by the way, as a birthday gift, may I have the bill for your car's tune-up?" he closed.

The weathered second-floor apartment I grew up in was updated with the shellacked veneer of knotty pine wainscoting from front room to back. In the center of the elongated layout was an outdated kitchen, squeezing in just enough room for a table with four place mats, five after my younger brother was born. Like clockwork, my father got home from work at five thirty in the evening. It took him twenty-five minutes to clean up and sit down for the dinner he expected at exactly six o'clock.

Every evening, we found our places around the table and waited for my father to sit down before we began to eat the meal my mother had prepared. This was our family ritual, devoid of prayer, greetings, or thanks. The dark circles on the knotty pine looked on in detached curiosity. Our conversation was slim until, after a few minutes, my father noticed my mother had done something he didn't like, or she had said something he thought was stupid, or she had forgotten something he had expected her to remember. Then the tirade began. He let her know in no uncertain terms what she had done wrong, and she defended herself, and he came back and put her down again. I blocked out the words to escape the cudgel, but he won—he always won.

When he was done eating, it meant dinner was over. He got up at precisely six twenty-five, went into the living room, sat in his big chair, and watched Walter Cronkite on the six thirty *CBS Evening News.* Night after night. Dinner after dinner. Fight after fight. When dinner was over, the drama was done.

Five months after I left the women's unit, I opened an envelope from my father that had arrived in the morning mail. My address was typed, so I knew my mother had done his bidding. Inside, there was no letter, just a newspaper article by Darrell Sifford, cut out of the *Philadelphia Inquirer.* The headline screamed, "Accusations of sex abuse, years later." It was a compendium of cases where daughters had accused their fathers of sexual abuse—falsely, according to the fathers—and a lament that the "sex abuse industry" was taking its toll on all-American families. This was the first of a number of articles he sent me on the issue of false memory syndrome, a movement to discredit dissociated memories.

I was not in a position to evaluate the truth of each article, but I was confused as to why my father was sending them. He and my mother had made it clear at our birthday party that abuse was not a topic for discussion, so I never brought it up to them again.

Where, I wondered, was my father's need to cure me of false memories coming from?

CHAPTER 7

SONIA

Moving with twelve-year-old Chuck and settling into our urban living environment slowed down my search for a new therapist. Jana had decided to move to New York, so I was committed to finding someone who would walk the walk with me. My flirtation with suicide and my hospitalization convinced me I couldn't make this journey without professional help. Still, planning daily lessons for my students, spending time with Chuck, and giving myself some space was important too, so I took my time before looking seriously.

Since Chuck was not entirely happy with the move, I found a male therapist for him before I found a therapist for myself. After school one afternoon, I arrived early to pick him up from his counseling session, sat down on the squeaky vinyl chair in the waiting room, and stared past the windowless walls. Presently, a nice-looking, soft, motherly kind of woman came out of the therapy area and looked around as if the person she expected wasn't there.

"No-show," she said, smiling, her British accent honey to my ears.

We murmured a few words to each other, and I told her I was looking for a new therapist. *She looks nice,* I thought. *Welcoming and warm. I like her British accent.* She seemed interested, so I said to her, "I'm new to the area and my son is in counseling with Tom Duprey. I'm a teacher—used to be the head of a school, but my whole life has been falling apart." *Her eyes are kind. She's listening to me.* I ventured forward.

"I've attempted suicide, I sometimes feel like I'm going crazy, and I admitted myself to the psychiatric hospital for a month last spring. I'm so afraid I might fall apart again, and I want to get to the bottom of this." *I wonder if I could work with her? I wonder if she could work with me?*

"Hmmm," she said. The waiting room walls disappeared as I focused entirely on how she responded to me.

"I need therapy that will help me do this. I don't want to be sad and crazy. I want to be happy and in control. But I don't know how to get there by myself."

"Hmmm." Sonia's demeanor seemed to reflect a sliver of light that landed directly in the center of my chest.

"Some people think I may have been sexually abused, but I don't have any memories," I added. *She doesn't seem to think I'm crazy.*

"Hmmm."

Could I trust her?

"Do you work with people like me?" *Oh, what the heck. I might as well take the bull by the horns and tell her everything. She doesn't seem to have anything else to do and she's listening.* "Sometimes I feel like a Survivor and sometimes I feel like a Victim." It poured out of me. "These parts of me even write in my journal. My father wrote me a letter and told me not to look for hobgoblins in the past. And not long ago, I had a twilight dream that told me I have a twin sister they gave away, but she is really me, and her name is Rosie. I don't have a twin sister and never did, and my parents never gave anybody away. I feel like I'm going crazy."

"Why don't we schedule a time to meet," the woman said softly but with a strength that drew me in. Without saying anything of substance, she sounded like she understood. She pulled out her appointment book and we set a time. *Whew. She hasn't run away. Maybe this will work.*

Trained in England as a clinical social worker, Sonia's tagline was "a psychoanalytically oriented psychotherapist." There were no bells and whistles in her therapeutic approach; rather, she just listened with a profound ear and responded. In the years to come, Sonia would listen and tell me I wasn't crazy. She would listen and tell me I was brave. She would listen and correct me when I said I was defective. She would listen and point out holes in my story when I took all the blame and defended someone who had hurt me. She would listen and gently guide me when I was really off the mark. She would listen to all the different voices that began to vie for airtime, and she would welcome each one with equal hospitality, even those who entered the therapy room angry and loaded for bear. She would listen and believe me, no matter what I said or how bizarre I sounded. When Sonia did probe, it was always couched in wonder: have you ever wondered . . . do you wonder . . . I wonder . . . to invite me to explore a topic more deeply.

Chuck never seemed to gel with Mr. Duprey, but that afternoon marked the beginning of a healing and transforming relationship for me with Sonia, my new therapist. We began with the easy stuff. The memories that were right on the top. Traumatic memories continued to wrack my body and confuse my mind without shape and form, but they could wait. I started with what I knew.

I was eight years old, kneeling on my bed, looking through the dusty slats of the faded blue-and-pink blinds of my bedroom window. From my spot peering through the narrow sashes, the street where our second-floor apartment sat seemed huge. I watched the cars on the busy two-lane highway go by at an even, easy pace. Our weathered apartment wasn't far from Philadelphia, and the small highway we lived on linked suburbs to city with our blue-collar town at the asphalt intersection between the two.

Bored, I jumped up and ran to the small window on the side-street wall of the bedroom where I could watch the men at the beer place. On the corner of the highway and a residential street, the sweaty workers at the distributor's warehouse worked day in and day out, driving the forklift truck that moved beer kegs from truck to storage to truck again.

When I grew older, I would have a crush on the man named Joe with big muscles, just like the other girls in the neighborhood who swooned over his masculinity.

My older sister, Kathy, and I shared the bedroom. She didn't like me much, so we barricaded ourselves on our personal sides of the bedroom, hers against the wall and mine near the small closet. On this particular day, she was out with friends, so I knew I could play her 33 1/3 rpm records on her phonograph player without getting into trouble. I listened to the soundtrack of *The South Pacific*, watching the disk go round and round, dreaming I was Nellie Forbush. I pulled out my stamp collection and checked my loose stamps against the stamp photos in my album. I had one prize stamp that looked like an anomaly according to my guidebook. Maybe I would get a lot of money for it. I didn't have any dolls, so I read books I had borrowed from the local library where I could walk by myself.

My father, mother, sister, brother, and I lived in a second-floor flat on a block where there were two taprooms, a beauty parlor, and a hobby shop. The first floor housed a little apartment where my paternal grandparents lived for many years and a small grocery store they managed in order to make ends meet. A big glass jar of candy sat on the counter, and I would walk downstairs twice each day to get my "morning's morning" and my "night's night." My father owned the whole corner building in this scrappy little neighborhood on the city's edge, and he established his parents beneath our apartment when they were unable to survive on their own.

The apartment was small, but big enough. Two bedrooms, a kitchen, living room and bathroom, with an extra bedroom where the stairwell met the entranceway. Below the two floors was a basement that was long, dark, and unfinished. The grown-ups had to bend their heads to avoid hitting the exposed water pipes draped with cobwebs. When I was very young, there was a tiny, makeshift room with a door right in the center of the basement. It housed my father's tools, but it disappeared sometime between my toddlerhood and pre-teen years. Outside our side door was a small shed about the same size as the toolroom. It also disappeared like a figment of someone's imagination.

My father was an electrician by trade and the maintenance superintendent at a large bank in the city. My mother was a stay-at-home mom, a poet, and a sometimes-depressed artist with real talent. I always figured we were poor, because we literally lived on the other side of the tracks, sewed our own clothes, rarely had the toys our friends had, and never took vacations.

My memory was never good. When I try hard, I can conjure up some happy moments of my childhood in this earthy and unvarnished neighborhood. When I try harder, the dark forebodings of a colicky, terrified little waif make their appearance. Mostly, my childhood was just a blank.

"When they brought you home from the hospital and started oohing and aahing over you, I knew this was NOT what I was expecting, so I turned and stomped out of the room," said my adult sister, Kathy, who was four years my senior and the sibling I'd shared a room with as a child. Not long after John and I separated, I drove north for a visit to her home in Vermont. Somehow, we got onto the topic of our childhoods, not a usual subject for us to explore. As she spoke, her body stiffened, and her face went flat with a frown. It didn't sound like she was recalling a childhood experience she had processed and grown through. Instead, it seemed like the telling of it brought her back into that distant space that was still alive and active in her inner world.

"I didn't want you; I didn't like you; in fact, I hated you," she growled, and I felt like I was back in our childhood home again. "So, I put you out of my life, ignored you, and pretended you weren't there. I did everything I could to make your life miserable." Her disdain was not limited to me; she was a Daddy's girl and treated my mother in much the same vein. "I felt the same way about Mom," she added. Both my mother and I were caught in the crosshairs of my sister's jealous wrath.

There was no exaggerating this extreme sibling rivalry that Kathy freely admitted to multiple times in the rare moments we shared as adults.

As a child, I experienced her commanding presence as imperial, as if she were the cruel queen and I were the submissive servant. There was no playing, no quiet talking in bed at night, no shared jokes or shared hopes and dreams because the queen, after all, can't be cavorting with a servant. I was a pariah, and that was that. The problem was, I loved her. I wanted her to love me. I would do anything to get her approval, but, like Charlie Brown's football, it was always pulled away just before I got there. The way she constantly ignored me all day every day, with no interludes of happy interaction in between, left me in a pool of pain that swept over me each time I was disappointed.

"Kathy, take your sister to the playground to play. You both need to get outside," my mother told Kathy one day when I was four years old. Kathy wasn't pleased with the assignment and had plans to play with her friends instead. Grudgingly, she left without so much as a glance while I hurried along behind, trying to catch up. We walked the two blocks to the sandstone elementary school, ran past the chain-link fence, and ran our hands along the metal rungs. She lost me when her long legs took the corners faster than my short ones, but I could see her from a distance. I found my way to the playground where she had climbed to the top of the sliding board to scan the horizon.

The battered and beaten-up swings, seesaws, merry-go-round, sliding board, and climbing bars were like Disneyland to me. I decided to try the swings and said, "Kathy, will you push me?" No answer. I climbed up by myself and tried pumping my legs in vain. When I got tired of that, I slid to the ground and stood up. "Kathy, come play with me on the merry-go-round." No answer. I ran over to the round wooden saucer, poised to spin fast enough to make me dizzy, sat down, and dangled my legs over the edge. Kathy's silence was deadening and told me all I needed to know.

Her friends arrived five minutes later, and they all burst into animated conversation. One of them looked at me and said, "Why don't we let Lyn be 'it'?"

"No. She's a nothing," Kathy replied. "Just ignore her." And so I was left alone on the merry-go-round, watching the big girls play, with no one offering a kind word or a friendly gesture. I never thought my sister's friends hated me, but they knew better than to cross her commands.

My relationship with my sister changed little in adulthood save for one two-year period when she lived in the same small-town college community in West Virginia where John and I lived. We became sisters then, walking, talking, and sharing a tentative but growing friendship. "I have two new students in my reading lab," she commented one morning as we walked up and down the hilly streets around my house. "They're advancing quickly. It makes me proud to see them do so well."

"Tell me how you work with them," I asked, genuinely curious to learn how to help struggling students. Kathy explained her approach in detail and agreed to come over for dinner that night and bring along some of her teaching materials for me to view. I got to know her as a real person during this period of our lives and admired her as well as loved her. She even attended Chuck's home birth, a truly blessed event. Sadly, we both moved from that town in different directions, and the old patterns set in again. Up until her death at the age of seventy-six as a retired, never-married, well-loved college professor, she held me at arm's length, and found her sisterhood in others in her life.

Kathy was unambiguous about her hatred of me, and I wondered why it was so extreme. To my knowledge, she never pursued that question herself.

⤳

Years before John and I divorced, my brother, Bob, who was eight years my junior, visited our family while on leave. "I hate the Army and I really don't want to re-up," he said. His first tour of duty was coming to a close, and he was struggling with this decision about his future.

"But I don't know what else to do. Daddy says I have to re-up. He doesn't think I can get a job. He's worried I won't be able to take care of myself." I spent some time acting as the older sister, exploring different options with him, including how he might support himself until he found a job.

Both my mother and father had been underestimating Bob to his face since he was born. They always said they couldn't expect much from Bob, that he'd never be able to keep up with others, that he would never manage on his own. Even as a young girl, I was uncomfortable with their lack of faith in their son—my brother—and how they conveyed this to him all day every day, which couldn't have added much to his self-esteem.

Now, years later, my father was trying to perpetuate his prophesy. I picked up the telephone and called him. "Dad," I said, "Bob just left. We had some good conversations about his future. He told me how much you want him to re-up, but he also said he didn't want to. He's not happy in the Army. We looked into some different options for him if he decides not to re-up, and I thought I would let you know."

"Damn you, Lynn," he shouted, and I knew I was in trouble. He only called me Lynn when he was mad at me. "He's not able to take care of himself. The Army will take care of him. Stay out of our business."

"Dad, I think you underestimate Bob. He's very capable. Maybe you could have more faith in his ability to manage his affairs."

"If he leaves the Army because of your meddling, I'll hold you responsible." My father slammed the phone down and wouldn't talk to me for months. I was interfering with his plans, and that infuriated him. As it was, Bob took a second tour of duty but decided to leave the Army at the end of it. He got a job in the postal service and worked his way up to technician. He was a smart man and a conscientious employee. He took care of my parents as their health declined, managed their affairs, and accumulated more financial stability than anyone in our family through his hard work and rigorous savings plan. He made something of himself, in spite of the fact that his parents didn't believe in him.

A year after my hospitalization, I was disowned.

My relations with my parents had been strained all year. I found I couldn't share anything of substance with them, and our connections were a distraction from the excruciating work of coping with my daily life. Communication with my father was difficult, and I began to see my mother as a victim—in thrall to my father, who was verbally and emotionally abusive to her. I think she desperately wanted me in her life, but she was unable to separate herself from my father. Essentially, they were one.

I, on the other hand, was tentatively trying out new skills of empowerment and independence I had learned in the hospital. I started setting boundaries. The very first time I set one, all hell broke loose.

"Hi, Mom. I'm so sorry to hear that Uncle Neil died. How are you doing?" My mother's brother, who lived in Louisiana, had died. They weren't close, but they were family. I wanted to know if she was okay. After discussing the sad circumstances, we made some small talk and I told her a little bit about my job, my emotional life, and my therapy.

"Yeah, life has been hard lately, but I'm so grateful for my therapist. She helps to keep me on track."

My mother's voice raised a pitch and she sounded tense. "Why are you in therapy? You really have to stop this."

I was taken aback that she would undermine the one thread that held me back from the brink. The tingling of danger coursed through my body, but I pushed through the shimmering icicles to stand my ground.

"Mom, I would appreciate it if you would not question my therapy. It's important for me, and if you can't support it, please just don't say anything."

She bellowed out her response in a way totally uncharacteristic for her.

"I just lost a brother and now I've lost a daughter!" Then she hung up the phone.

As I look back on it, my mother was probably gripped by grief, but I too was dealing with my own form of grief. I took her statement to mean she was disowning me. When Thanksgiving came and I wasn't invited but my ex-husband was, that confirmed her intention. While I was terrified by the estrangement, I was also relieved. I wrote in my journal, *Without a family, I feel lost. Maybe I've always been without a family. I just didn't know it before.* Suicidal ideation, which I never acted on again, was always just under the surface. *Take it away. Take away this pain or take away my life.*

Being disowned was a gift. It gave me the freedom and space to do the work I needed to do, away from the toxic family environment. I found I didn't miss them, but I did, at times, feel like I was floating in outer space without the anchor family usually provides. As time went on, I might receive a card from my mother or father, which I usually ignored, largely because their relationship with John continued to flourish. From what I could see, John became the brilliant, high-achieving son my father had always wanted, forming a cohesive family unit whose purpose was, in part, to keep me sidelined. Family holidays went by with my father, mother, ex-husband, and children celebrating without me. The whole idea that my parents would nurture a relationship with the man who had betrayed me stopped me in my tracks if I ever thought about reconciling. Life was too hard as it was to add any other drama or obstacle.

Yet I learned the power of boundaries. Setting boundaries—an essential step in getting healthy—was anathema in my family.

Believing in God did not take away my pain or turn my life around. I continued to descend into the depths of my craziness and work through the pieces bit by bit. It did, however, give me an anchor that moored me in my most dire moments, and the hope that what goes down will eventually come up again out of the pit.

In the earliest days of my decompensation before my acknowledgment of faith, I found myself praying in spite of myself: *God, give me strength and wisdom. God, give me strength and wisdom.* I had no idea my prayers would be answered; I simply prayed the same prayer over and over again because the very act of praying kept me alive. After about a year, I realized I was getting stronger and smarter. Truly, I thought, the God-that-didn't-exist was answering my prayers.

When I was in the psychiatric hospital, I learned the serenity prayer: *God grant me the serenity to accept the things I cannot change, the courage to change the things I can, and the wisdom to know the difference.* This prayer has been the bedrock for people with addictions for decades. Living in Bethlehem alone, I took that prayer and changed it to suit my needs: *God grant me the courage, strength, and wisdom to know myself and do your will.* I needed courage to face the unfaceable, strength to keep going every day, and wisdom to uncover the complicated machinations of my mind. I needed to discover who I was, both angel and demon, and everything in between.

Ultimately, I asked that this process would lead me in a way that was pleasing to the God-I-was-just-discovering. I prayed this prayer constantly, year after year, at home in my journal, in school when I was teaching my students, anywhere when I was in the middle of a trigger, in my heart as I tentatively reached out to my real children who were carrying burdens of their own, in fear as I confronted the worst of me. It was my prayer without ceasing, an ancient form of petition.

God grant me the courage, strength, and wisdom to know myself and do your will.

Initially, my faith was fluid without much form. I continued to be wary of religious folks who put God in a box and told me what to believe. I was more comfortable with "letting go and letting God" as I walked this unfamiliar territory. I read voraciously but never pushed myself to believe, act, or feel something that wasn't coming to me naturally.

I began to trust myself because I was trusting in something greater than myself. Slowly, my need for hard evidence was replaced by my very own experiential evidence. I didn't need scientific proof of the existence of God because God was an undeniable felt presence that was always with me. Prayer offered me the experience of God even when my mind couldn't believe in God.

From my new apartment in Bethlehem, I could walk downtown, past the quaint shops, over a small bridge and through a stand of trees to Sand Island in the middle of the Lehigh River that flowed through the city. Walkers and joggers would sprint past me as I strolled leisurely past the children who were climbing the playground equipment, laughing and calling out to their parents. I kept walking until I came to the end of the little island where the water lapped up on the sand and the landscape framed the old, defunct Bethlehem Steel across the river, a skeleton of what it used to be. I loved sitting there, taking in the contrast of nature and manmade artifice. Trees, brush, river, steel—I thought they were all beautiful, even the old industry, which held the very human hope of prosperity a century ago. Somehow, together, they embodied a grace that buoyed me. Breathing in the imagery and breathing out my pain was prayer enough.

Over the next decade, I delved into the depths of my being with Sonia, who helped me give birth to myself. Eight of those years included one and a half hours of individual therapy and one and a half hours of group therapy each week. Although she was only a few years older than me, she felt like the blessed mother, a font of wisdom and a paten of love. She was ordinary in stature, of average build, with shoulder-length brown hair. What made her so unique were her eyes that reflected fathomless compassion, and her presence, which provided an unaccustomed net of safety. I fell in love the first time I sat down with her.

In one of our early sessions, Sonia asked me to tell her what I remembered about my family. I was in control as I sat upright in a big, overstuffed, white leather chair. My thoughts went immediately to my father, and I began to describe him.

"When I was very little, maybe three or four years old," I began, "my father sang songs to me while putting me to bed." I recalled the image fondly. "He would cuddle and bounce me on his knee and tickle me," I continued. "He took baths with me, but I barely remember that." My mind went blank. "As I grew up, I watched him with other little children; he loved to cuddle and play with them too." I felt confused. "When I grew older, he became more aloof and distant, stern and controlling, the family dictator." I shivered and sank deep into the stuffing of the chair.

"I respected my father more than I loved him."

"That must have been sad to respect your father more than love him," Sonia said. "All children need to love and be loved." In the folds and among the neurons of my deadened awareness, a snake-like consciousness slithered over every syllable Sonia said, trying to separate truth from lie, searching for a safe space. *Can I trust her?* Her words oozed over my unresponsive mind like mineral oil. She asked a few more questions, and I answered as I could.

Then I stopped talking. I sat for a few minutes with my eyes closed, totally unaware of the therapeutic environment around me, the long orange couch next to my chair, the floral framed print on the wall above it, the shaded glass window behind me, Sonia in her brown therapy chair across from me. Instead, I was in a vast sea of blank, a dry desert devoid of life, waiting, waiting. I yawned. A small voice crept out. *"I am a little baby. In a crib. I am not happy. He is there. I don't like him. I am not very good. I am very very bad."*

"Is this Rosie?" asked Sonia softly. I froze. I couldn't answer. I didn't know. Waiting some more, I yawned again, my eyes still closed. *"It is too confusing. I am too many people at one time. I don't know who to listen to. On top of it all, it hurts. I hurt. My body is in pain. I'm exhausted. All I want to do is die."* I yawned again. More waiting. *"No, that's not true. All I want to do is live."* Yawn. Silence. I opened my eyes. Sonia was still there, watching me closely with gentle eyes.

I smiled and stretched. In the nothingness of my mind, several *switches* had occurred, the term used to describe moving from one dissociative part to another, although I didn't, in the moment, know what switches were, that I was having them, or that my yawns were a signal that I had switched. Sonia didn't push me to go beyond my comfort level. I left her office confused, my body wracked with pain, but feeling perversely good. My heart burned light, my eyes filled with water, and my body resonated like the ringing of a tuning fork. I hurt, but it was a good hurt. I left the session knowing something important had happened but not sure of the meaning.

As time went on, I learned that Rosie was tiny, maybe two or three years old, and didn't say much. Her core characteristic was trust. She never revealed who "he" was, but, even when he hurt her, she would crawl back onto his lap and trust again. Her trust and her fears were woven together into a cord that had kept her tied up for many years. She was ready to be released, and our work with Sonia began to cut the cord. Still, my cognitive mind resisted believing Rosie was anything more than a figment of my imagination. I was making her up, I was sure. For years, I existed in the intersection between belief and disbelief that Rosie and the others I would meet were any more than flights of fancy.

Through Sonia's deep listening and profound questions and comments, Rosie discovered someone who was trustworthy, the snake who seemed to reside in my mind found a safe space by slithering intentionally over Sonia's every word, and the tuning fork that took a read on my condition began to ring each time we touched on something important.

CHAPTER 8

DIAGNOSED

One day, after sketching out reading plans for the next two weeks, a voice coopted my journal and complained, *I am the one who takes care of Rosie. My name is Nanny, and I don't like it,* she said with the authority of a full-time caregiver. *I don't want to do this,* she added, referring to teaching children in a classroom. *It's too hard. I'm too exhausted. Rosie takes a lot of energy. When she slides off his lap, she's like a limp washrag. I'm depleted. Those children* (in the classroom) *have more energy than me. They will overcome me. Besides, why should I put energy into them? I want to put it into Rosie. She needs me. Those kids are taking energy from Rosie.*

By this time, I was teaching an adjunct class at a local college in addition to my fulltime first-grade teaching position. Somehow, Nanny absorbed all of Rosie's pain, a dynamic that enabled Rosie to trust again through a never-ending loop of trauma survival: Rosie trusts, Rosie hurts, Nanny holds Rosie's pain so Rosie can trust again. Nanny, unfortunately, was left with the exhausted, emaciated body, barely able to function.

By contrast, when I was in the classroom, I was fine. Other parts of me I had not yet met took over and managed all my professional duties. The more I taught, the less I felt exhausted in the moment, affirming yet again the power of the front brain to pick up the pieces when the *limbic system*, the technical term for the back brain in all its many functions, was in trauma mode.

All these jobs are too much, Nanny complained. I imagined her as a haggard old woman who was exhausted by her role as caretaker. She continued, *At least when you were married, you could stay home and take care of Rosie. Now I'm stuck with the job. Well, you could make it easier for me by staying home. Then I could give Rosie my full attention.* Nanny might be pushing Rosie in a stroller or comforting her hurting body in a rocking chair, all in my inner world. It took a toll on her as she carried all the exhaustion that I couldn't afford to carry myself because of my real-world commitments. She also felt a lot of fear and impending doom.

I'm sick to my stomach and my body is tense, Nanny pleaded and begged. *I'm exhausted but I'm scared. What if I can't do this? I might die. Rosie might die. We all might die. Don't you see? I'm the only one who sees this. We might die. Don't ask me why. I don't know. I just know.* In fight, flight, or freeze mode, Nanny was frozen.

Now that our three realities—mine, Rosie's, and Nanny's—were comingled as one, I carried their experiences with me. When Rosie was trusting, I was trusting. When her trust was misplaced, I was devastated. When every pore of Nanny screamed catatonia, my every pore wanted to curl up into that fetal position I had become so familiar with in the past ten years. Like Thelma, I was co-conscious, which meant I had few amnesic barriers between my parts. Now I sensed who the despair belonged to and had an inkling of what it was about.

Although Nanny and Rosie explained some of my pain and angst, they didn't account for other experiences that checkered my life. Why was there still a veil separating me from my real children? How could I walk into the classroom with enthusiasm, confidence, and not a shred of tiredness? What about the other voices and internal nudges?

~

Triggers are minor events in the present that awaken a disproportionate emotional or bodily response to a trauma from the past. They are a kind of memory in and of themselves—not visual memory but visceral, emotional, bodily memory, at the least. Memory experts say they tap into an uninterrupted loop that links the present stimulus with the unprocessed memory from the past. The stimulus is the trigger that propels the person into a memory-based response that has not been processed, healed, or outgrown.

Prior to hospitalization, I lived in one big, dissociative bubble. Now that I was engaged in deep work with Sonia, I began to recognize individual triggers and know when I had entered a triggered state. As in the past, I would be all-consumed by emotions that no talk-down could puncture. As in the past, my body felt raw. Now, with regular therapeutic processing, my thoughts often became labored as I picked apart what had happened and how I was responding all at the same time. Gradually, I might sense that I wasn't entirely rational, and slowly, usually over a twenty-four-hour period, I would come out of the frightening dissociative state.

At first, most of my identified triggers propelled me into victimhood.

When Lizzy talked back to me, I crawled into a fetal position and felt confused, impotent, and terrified. I was a terrible mother. I loved my daughter with all my heart, but her disobedience proved I was defective.

When John fought for his rights in the divorce settlement, I had no wherewithal to fight back, no sense of entitlement myself, so I gave in and pulled the covers over my head. Some part of me actually thought I deserved nothing and assumed John was justified in withholding from me.

When another teacher said something that could be construed as critical, I became terrified she had discovered I was a fake and imposter. I would take these and other triggers to Sonia for help in wading through the powerful emotions I was having.

"Did you ever think she might be jealous when she said that?" Sonia might ask.

"Jealous? Why would she be jealous?"

"Because you're so good at what you do."

"Really?" And so it went that Sonia's delicate suggestions would help me reevaluate the situation that had triggered me and help me respond in more appropriate and effective ways.

Underneath the victimhood, however, a new emotion began to emerge. Anger. The privacy of my journal gave me voice to express this forbidden feeling with abandon. In strong, bold lettering I would spew my juvenile wrath on the offending person.

I HATE her!
I HATE him!
Fucking person! How dare he/she!
Dumb, stupid, hate, hate, hate!!!

Now, I myself was not stupid. I knew I couldn't openly share the feelings a person elicited in me, whether that was rage, fear, despair, or even affection that was not proportionate to the situation. I slowly learned that while my basic instinct was often on target, the magnitude of the feeling was usually not. And on occasion, my instinct failed me altogether and I was way off base. So, for many of my therapy years, I delayed my responses to other people and took them to Sonia to process my emotions and get a reality check on the substance of the situation.

Lizzy talked back? Yes, that's what teenagers do sometimes. You aren't a victim. Go ahead and scream and rage in the therapy room and in your journal. Then you can get out of bed and go back in there and be a parent. John wants more money? Well, that's what ex-husbands do sometimes. They want to protect their own assets. Crying and trembling will help you shake off your fear. Then, you can fight for your rights just like he fights for his. The teacher next door made a snide remark? That's her problem. Journal as much as you want, then keep doing what you're doing. Eventually, you'll learn how to let it roll off your back.

This delayed response was a cumbersome process that continued through my teaching at two different schools, and while I went to graduate school for school administrator certification and became a principal at a 550-student public elementary school. As my career took off, the stakes were higher and the triggers more frequent. Power and authority terrified me. I knew that without processing my emotions and taking a reality check on the situation, I would sabotage myself.

The challenge was discovering the original events that gave rise to the triggered response. I eventually learned the difference between *implicit traumatic memory* and *explicit cognitive memory*. When an event occurs, it is channeled through the back emotional brain where the *amygdala* acts as a fire alarm. If there's no perceived danger, the event is sent to the front brain where rational thought occurs and stored as an explicit narrative-based memory. If danger is present, the event never makes it to the front brain and, instead, is immediately sent into the body to initiate a fight, flight, or freeze response. The memory residue of repeated trauma is called implicit memory and may or may not include some unconnected narrative fragments. This is exactly what I was experiencing—the telltale signs of events that seemed to be lost to my conscious mind—but I didn't know it at the time. I wanted rock-solid memories I could take to the bank.

I never wanted to be crazy. Almost from the beginning of my decompensation, when I had the energy to think about it, I wanted to be sane and normal, with a shot at happiness, just like other people. For me, that meant that I would resume a life without a myriad of voices, without an endless stream of pain, without feeling like a victim, without the sense of unreality that so often enveloped me. Instead, my sense of self would be unified and integrated, my bonds with my real children would be renewed, I would have a loving relationship with another human being, and I would no longer be a victim. I would be a survivor, a thriver. I would own my own power and leave my pervasive sense of powerlessness behind.

Not surprisingly, relationships became a major theme in my therapy with Sonia. In my nuclear and family of origin, as well as with friends beyond my family, I had difficulties with intimate relationships because they required trust. Even though I thought I trusted people, I didn't. My presenting part might put on a good show, but the rest of my *system*—the common term for the interaction of alters in one person—had a different story to tell.

"How often did you blame others for your problems?" shot John in a seven-page typed letter excoriating me during the height of our breakup. He listed everyone whom he thought I had blamed for a whole truckload of sins. He twisted stories and included many mischaracterizations, but there was some truth in his observation. With the exception of Thelma, I didn't know how to have friends, I didn't know how to navigate complicated interpersonal waters, and I had a hidden lack of trust in other people. I was good at faking it, and other people saw me as a social, happy, friendly, capable person. This deep-seated trust issue was well hidden, even from me.

Once I began therapy with Sonia, my internal radar kept drawing me into therapeutic and real-life situations that challenged this pathology. Faith in a God who loved me just the way I was didn't require a lot of intimacy, at least not at first. Connecting in Quaker meeting so I could watch how people interacted from a distance gave me a good idea of what "normal" looked like. Going to group therapy, in spite of huge triggers, got to the meat of the matter. Allowing each voice to come out and speak their truth to Sonia gave me more and more confidence in my real relationships. It wasn't easy; in fact, it was excruciating, but my system kept thrusting me into situations that forced me to confront my dysfunctional perceptions.

The world is built on relationships. If I was to have any semblance of a normal, sane life, I had to move beyond my doubt, fear, and shame and learn how to be vulnerable and intimate. I fully expected memories would emerge to explain away the craziness I was experiencing but, in the meantime, I focused on learning how to trust appropriately and navigate relationships.

I began to attend a new Quaker meeting when I moved to Bethlehem. One Sunday afternoon, I wrote in my journal, *Meeting was nice this morning. It is a grounding place for me. A bit distant, which is okay. But a place to see people who connect with me. To see that I am like other people. I am different, but not so different. Bright, strong people at meeting are vulnerable like me. A centering place. A grounding place. I think I am accepted and valued there too.*

Because my mind usually functioned well even when my feelings were all jumbled up, I found myself studying and reading about Quakers, or the Religious Society of Friends as they are formally known. Staying in my head touched my heart without requiring me to develop intimate relationships, which always ran the risk of hurting me. I could grow spiritually without jeopardizing my emotional safety. Gradually, I put my little toe into meeting by joining a ministry committee. We met at the home of Martha, a woman I knew through graduate school. One evening, I was agitated by something unrelated to the committee and broke down in tears. I was horrified. I was being vulnerable in front of people I hardly knew. I always tried to project strength, but here I was, letting down my guard and showing weakness.

"I'm so sorry. I shouldn't be crying. Please forgive me. I'm usually strong. Sorry," I gasped, trying to regain control. Martha stood, walked around the table to where I was sitting, and put her arms around me.

"Lyn, we don't love you because you're strong. We love you because you're you."

Wow. I wasn't expecting that. Here was real compassion and no expectation that I had to be strong. I wasn't ready to reveal all to these people—and that was sensible—but I learned that I could show weakness and still be safe and valued as a person.

A year after my hospitalization, I was forty-five years old and struggling with a diagnosis. This little three-year-old waif named Rosie was in the center of my chaos, and the part of me who called herself

Nanny claimed to be the one taking care of her. On top of that, other parts were popping out all over the place, claiming names and demanding a voice in my conscious mind. However, I was a smart, accomplished woman, and I didn't buy any of it. I was sure it was all an invention of my imagination, which, I would learn later, is a clear sign of dissociative identity disorder, sometimes dubbed the "hidden disorder" since its very purpose is to hide the abuse from everyone, including the one who owns it. Yet as preposterous as it sounded, having insiders or alters resonated with a deep, visceral part of me, the part of me that felt, that spewed raw, uncensored words on a page, that curled into a fetal ball on a regular basis, that lived in fear almost every second of every day.

Still, the functioning, cognitive part didn't believe myself for a minute. I wrote in my journal, *I know you can tell I am having a hard time with this. It isn't easy. You know I don't want to pretend. I know some of this is real, but some of it seems like make-believe. I don't want to make something up. I want to get well, to get healthy. Are you there? Will you help me?*

Or:

I am not a multiple personality, but I am screwed up and very confused. If I forget about names and just talk about feelings, then it will be okay.

On good days, I cut myself a break.

I'm here, I told whomever was there, if anyone. *When you're ready, I'm here. I care about you. I want us to be partners, allies. I know it's rough now, for all of us. It's confusing and scary, but I want you to know I'm here. And even though other people are important to me, you are most important. I want you to come first. No one, and nothing, is more important than you.* Even though my real children were the most important to me, I knew I needed to put myself first, which meant prioritizing the alters I didn't believe existed. *I may feel sick, I may be complaining, but that's because I'm confused. It's okay. It's okay for me to feel sick if that's what I have to do to get to know you. That's how important you are to me. I accept it. I accept you.*

Rosie and Nanny didn't go away. Others began to make themselves known. "Tell me, Sonia, what do you think?" I asked her, frantic, terrified to know the answer. "Do you believe that multiple personalities exist? Do you think I have multiple personalities? I think it's crazy, but I need to know what you think." Throughout my years of therapy, Sonia submitted my diagnosis as post-traumatic stress disorder, an accepted diagnosis that an insurance company would cover. On the other hand, multiple personality disorder was controversial and sure to raise the scrutiny of the claim's office. Nonetheless, she forged ahead.

"Yes, Lyn," she replied, "I believe there's such a thing as multiplicity, and I believe you are multiple. What's really important, though, is what you think." I needed to hear her say that, but I still didn't believe it. I decided to get a second opinion from a psychiatrist affiliated with Northwestern Institute. I prayed fervently, *Who am I? Lord, please let me be one person. How can I live a sane life with myself and others if I am not one person, whole and together? Who am I?*

The days leading up to that appointment were tumultuous. Multiple voices vied for airtime, frightened, ashamed, confused. This new doctor was a threat. He wouldn't believe me. He'd tell me I was bad or crazy. I was going to get into trouble.

I'm a bad girl.

He's going to tell me I'm a bad girl.

But don't hurt me.

Nothing.

I'm bad for thinking these things. I'm bad for writing them. He will tell me that. He will tell me that it isn't true. He will tell me to go home and buckle up and get better. But he won't say it like that. He will make it sound nice and supportive and professional and true. And I will go home and believe him and disappear.

I think I've tricked everyone.

I've tricked Sonia.

I've tricked the therapy group.

I've tricked my friends.

I've tricked myself.

Tomorrow night he will discover that I've tricked everyone.

And he will tell me that I'm bad because I have tricked them.

After school on a crisp fall Monday afternoon, I drove an hour into Philadelphia to meet with this new psychiatrist. On the way, an unfamiliar part of me took the wheel. She was alive and happy and began to have strong sexual feelings.

I can feel energy in every part of my body. It's electric. I'm electric. The space between my legs was quivering and sending signals everywhere, making it difficult to concentrate on driving. *Oh, wow. I love this! Watch out. You have to drive. Be careful. Oooh, I can't wait to meet this new doctor. Maybe he's handsome. Maybe we can have some fun. Check the directions. Turn the corner. He can't hurt us. Let's do it!* This part knew how to take care of the new doctor—she wanted to seduce him. Later, she would tell me her name was Sylvia.

When we got to the doctor's office, Sylvia dutifully retreated into the background and let Lyn go into the session. I remember little of what happened except that after I'd told the doctor what was going on, he said he saw little reason to doubt what my own body, mind, and spirit were telling me. He confirmed the diagnosis.

I could no longer deny my reality. I had multiple personalities, as it was called back then. Rosie, Nanny, Sylvia, and others were real parts of me. I was afraid but also relieved. At least there was an explanation for my chaotic consciousness.

One afternoon, while peeling apart my emotions, I collapsed in Sonia's office, crying, "I am so defective! I'm either happy or miserable or terrified or angry or confused or numb. I'm so crazy to be so jumbled up with emotions, sometimes all at the same time. I can't begin to know what I, Lyn, am feeling when I don't even know who's feeling them. There are so many emotions, conflicting emotions, emotions that don't make sense, and sometimes no emotion at all. What's wrong with me?!"

I sobbed and sobbed and barely heard Sonia through my tears.

"Lyn, everything everybody feels is okay, valid, and important."

What? Say that again?

"Everything everybody feels is okay, valid, and important."

I was stunned. That simple message struck a powerful chord that echoed deeply through the caverns of my aching body.

It's okay? I said to myself slowly, in awe. *All my feelings are okay? Did you hear that? Hey, everybody inside, our feelings are okay. Not only that, they're valid and important,* I went on, picking up speed. *Did you hear Sonia say that? No matter how nutsy I feel, no matter how nutsy WE feel, I'm okay and we're okay!*

I walked out of the therapy office that day with a new sense of rightness, a calmness that came from hearing someone affirm my feelings, all of them. Lightness lifted my body as I closed Sonia's door. The dull throb of pain that usually followed me scattered on the sidewalk from her office to my car. I turned on the ignition with my heart twice as big as it usually was. My lips shaped a smile that I couldn't conceal if I wanted to. As soon as I got home, I typed a fancy poster on my primitive Apple Macintosh computer so I wouldn't forget those profound words. With a new, tentative confidence, I printed it out and hung it on my refrigerator. Bordered with hearts and with a heart in the center, it said, *Everything everybody feels is okay, valid, and important.*

The next week, Chuck and I made a cake for Kimmy, who was visiting on her sixteenth birthday. In a few days, the American voters would elect Bill Clinton as president, but we were more interested in celebrating a family victory. The three of us gathered in my first-floor kitchen in the Bethlehem apartment, laughing, playing games, and talking about everyone's circumstances. I didn't overlook the fact that the poster affirming my feelings hanging on my refrigerator door was also an affirmation of Kimmy's and Chuck's feelings, and the backdrop for our reunion.

"Kimmy, how are you feeling on your sixteenth birthday?" I asked my daughter, who was going through her own challenging times.

"I'm great." She smiled and took another bite of cake.

I would never forget Sonia's simple sentence. Wrinkled and smeared

with kitchen blots and stains, that poster is still with me to this day.
Everything everybody feels is okay, valid, and important.

Over the years, new voices emerged as I went deeper and deeper
into my psyche. During my second year post-hospitalization, I dreamed
about the Protector. He embodied the old-man-in-the-sky image of
God with long white hair, a white robe, and an angelic expression.
Because he was kind and gentle, I thought he was God.

"Sonia, I met God in a dream the other night. His name is
Protector, and he made all my alters."

"That's wonderful, Lyn, but I don't think that was God. I think
Protector is an alter who helped you by creating other alters when you
needed them."

I didn't believe Sonia at first and much preferred the idea that
Protector was God. Or a guardian angel. I liked the idea that the
Divine might have intervened personally in my trauma. It put a sort
of imprimatur on my system. *I am your protector, Lyn. I am god-like,
but I am not God,* Protector told me. *I am in the image of your father,
but unlike him, I am good. I came to be at about the same time as Rosie.
Actually, a little before Rosie. I could see you needed help, so I created her.*
I couldn't refute Protector's own voice, so I relented. He was not God,
but he may have been a guardian angel. So God did intervene, just not
in the way I had imagined.

I asked Protector if he knew the details of abuse. *Yes, I know
everything,* he said. *But I will never tell. You couldn't handle it. I will take
care of you. I always have. Don't you remember? I am the one who whispers
"I love you" in your ear. It is my arms you feel holding you, wrapped gently
around your body. I will protect you.*

I sensed Protector's presence everywhere even though he wasn't
active in the ways my other alters were. He was just there, watching,
waiting, loving, ready to step in when I needed help. When I became
uncomfortable with male oversight, Protector was willing to change

genders. When I wrote a plan for another attempt at suicide, Sonia required me to sign a promise that I would visit her in person three times before acting on any plan, and Protector stepped in and dissuaded me from carrying it out. When most holidays were excruciating for me, Protector made sure that Christmas was always wonderful.

Christmas is my Father's birthday, he explained, *and I arrange it so we are all stable, relaxed, and reasonably happy. I am stabilizing you now,* he assured me mid-December during the early days of my recovery. *You are okay. You will have a good Christmas.* To this day, Christmas has always been a peaceful holiday, a legacy of Protector, who celebrated the birth of God in me.

CHAPTER 9

"WORK"

E very week, I "worked" with Sonia. Dedicating every ounce
of myself to the task of uncovering and recovering was hard
labor. I began my sessions with traditional talk therapy where I
brought issues I'd encountered during the week and began to talk about
them. There was always plenty to choose from, whether I described
some internal emotional challenge, processed interactions with the
outside world, or grabbed for sanity after a trigger. Although I began
with sixty-minute sessions, it quickly became clear that to follow my
natural rhythm to a place of minimal closure, I needed an hour and a
half at a time. Sonia was willing to oblige.

Sonia had an open policy for midweek phone calls. If a part of
me was in crisis, I was to call and leave a message; she would get back
to me as soon as she could. Her purpose was to nurture trust among
my insiders, who weren't about to give much away to a once-a-week
therapist. I tried not to abuse that offer but sometimes picked up the
phone in debilitating terror, calling for a reality check or just to hear
the sound of her voice, which had the capacity to calm me.

Over time, parts of me began to talk when I was in the therapy room.
I would close my eyes, grow quiet, silent, still. A yawn was indicative
of a switch as I moved from myself to an alter, or from one alter to
another. In this liminal space, I usually felt nothing. Eventually, out of
the nothingness a voice would emerge.

"Help me, oh help me, please," said Rosie in a little voice. *"I am just a little girl in here. And there are so many ways big people hurt me. Please help me. I am scared. I am so afraid."*

"You're safe here," said Sonia gently. "Can you tell me more?"

"There is a corner in the basement," Rosie continued.

"Yes I know," some other part of me responded.

"There is a corner in the basement."

"Yes, I know."

"Cold and dusty and awful and safe. It's where I went to get away. Cold and dusty and awful and safe."

"I am making all of this up," I interrupted. "I don't know any of this. It's just popping into my mind." My eyes were still closed.

"There are tunnels in my basement," Rosie went on, speaking through my body. *"Not really but in my mind. When we go to the toolshed, I crawl through them. And I am scared. And even now I am scared of tunnels."* Rosie's eyes were heavy laden, afraid to open and take in the present day. *"I am afraid I will get caught and I will never get out. Little teeny spaces, crawl spaces, cold and dark and dusty and safe. When I crawl there in my mind, I'm safe from him."*

My body was limp, and my eyes still closed as Rosie continued. *"I am scared. I am very scared. There is a black hole. It is my throat. It is my mind. I am afraid of the hole. I am afraid to get closer to that hole. I don't want to look inside. I don't want to know what's inside. I am so afraid."* I sat silently for a few more minutes. No more words came. Little tears trickled down Rosie's face. She was limp. I was limp. It was over. Just as Nanny had described, Rosie/I felt like a limp washrag when it was done.

"Thank you for sharing, Rosie," Sonia said. "You are brave. I hope you come back and talk again." The snake in my brain listened to Sonia's words carefully, trying to discern what they meant and whether Rosie would be safe now that she had spilt some of the beans. The verdict was still out as he slithered back into his hole. I rose from the chair in Sonia's office and felt the tuning fork ring.

It was dangerous to be angry around my father.

One day when I was about ten years old, I tripped over my little brother's plastic tow truck in our cramped living room. As I fell, my knee hit the edge of a wooden chair and it hurt. I saw red. The tow truck was nearby, so I picked it up and threw it to the floor in frustration.

When my father saw me express anger, he was furious. "Don't you ever do that again," he yelled as he grabbed my arm and dragged me through the house to his bedroom. There, he brandished my mother's hairbrush and began pummeling me. I crumbled under the wrath of his rage and the impact of the brush, four, five, six times. My skin was swollen red and tender, with streaks of blood under the surface. When it was over, I crept into my own room, heaving quiet sobs, and hid underneath the thin cotton covers of my bed. I was accustomed to his method of disciplining—not a raging, out-of-control beating but a deliberate, hardcore, this-is-what-happens-when-you-step-out-of-line punishment.

So, over time and into adulthood, I forgot about anger. I knew it was dangerous to get angry, so why bother? Instead, I was good, nice, pliable, and always forgiving. Not only that, I had a natural tendency to want everyone to like me. On personality tests, I was the nurturer and peacemaker. In real life, I was the one who bent over backwards to make sure I said nice things to people even when I needed to correct or direct them. Sometimes, I think, I sent mixed messages to people because I was afraid they wouldn't like me.

A crucial part of my healing was getting in touch with the part of me who held the anger and then using my anger to propel me toward healing. It began with journaling, which gave me cover to express what I was really feeling. No one would ever read it, except Sonia, and I was starting to trust her. With a tentative sense of safety, I began to explore the forbidden feelings I had stuffed for years. At first, I expressed diffuse anger at everyone and no one in my writing, ranting and railing without a particular target in mind. Then I would focus on a person or situation from my past, spewing out rage between lines on a page. The hardest transition was learning how to get angry with someone in the here and now. That presented a lot of hurdles I had to overcome.

Sometimes I got furious at Sonia as a way of testing my anger and testing her. I found I could do it, and she let me.

"Sonia, I hate you, I hate you, I hate you. You're mean and miserable. I don't like you."

"Tell me more, Lyn. What's really going on?" And so it went, me venting emotional memories, and Sonia listening and helping me process them.

My big breakthrough came when Mike introduced himself. He was Sylvia's teenaged twin, and he rumbled through my being into my journal, into the therapy room, and into my day-to-day interactions with real people who wondered where this new feistiness was coming from.

"It's none of your business who I am!!! I am me, and that's all there is to it," he roared in response to Sonia's question about his identity. *"I feel a rod of steel growing inside my body. It says, don't mess with me. Don't mess with me. Friends, enemies, strangers, ex-husbands, parents, children, therapists . . . Don't Mess With Me!"*

Although Mike's grand entrance was threatening and filled with rage, he ultimately had the good of my system at heart. He cared about me and about every part of me. He wanted me to succeed, to be whole, and for my whole system to function well. Thus, he criticized, with a keen eye, every twist and turn of my life.

I am not pleased with the turn that therapy is taking, he opined. *I don't want to be a fucking victim. I don't want to sit around with a bunch of women, trying to figure out how I was victimized. But I do. But I don't. Just help me get better and I won't need to do that. I was a victim, but I'm not now. I. Am. Not. Now.*

I actually felt Mike expand in my body, a phenomenon he explained readily.

That steel rod is growing. I can feel it in my body. It goes right down my torso and into my arms and legs. It's not in my head yet. It originates from a place in the center of my chest near my heart. Fuck it. Fuck everything that hurts, that is painful. That steel rod protects me. Fuck therapy. Soon I won't need it. The steel rod will make me strong.

As angry as he was, he was quick and smart, thinking things through from his teenage perspective. *I'm a little worried about what will happen when the steel rod goes into my head,* he reflected. *A steel rod is pretty inflexible. I want my mind to be tough as steel, but flexible. I want the steel rod to melt and form delicate but tough pins that can be fastened together with hinges so that my mind is tough but flexible.* And just like that, Mike willed the form his strength would take—not rigid and inflexible but agile and tough.

Over time, Mike's anger was the source of deep healing for me. His relentless drive to make our whole system healthy endowed him with the leadership my fragmented system needed. When I wanted to die, he took the reins and walked me through whatever crisis was before me. To keep me calm, he rocked my small child parts when they cried or were in distress. Like a cowboy herding disparate beasts going in many different directions, he herded my insiders and led me to the water hole. To use his language, Mike was fucking pissed off that circumstances had pulled my life off track, and he was willing to do anything he could to steer me straight. He was sure I deserved to have a life, even when I was sure I didn't.

Through Mike, I befriended anger and learned how to use it to my advantage without hurting anyone else. I lost my fear of anger and embraced the good it could do when channeled appropriately. I rode the coattails of my anger into a new, productive, and peaceful life—but not until Mike got his fury out.

I ran into the bathroom of the professional building quickly and slammed the cubicle door behind me as every pore of my sexuality throbbed with an aching desire that had to be satisfied right then and there. *Is this me? I can't believe I'm doing this.* A look, a thought, and a smile in the meeting room all sent the message with perfect timing that opened me up and sent my juices flowing. *Ooh, I need this so badly.*

I threw my bag on the door hook and put my work materials on the back of the toilet while one hand caressed my breast and the other felt for the soft flesh between my legs. *Who cares who this is? Just do it.* Slow rhythmic movement up and down, back and forth, slowly, slowly, slowly, now more quickly, now more deeply, now more intimately. *More. I need more.* My mind raced through a fantasy seduction to heighten the intensity, the desire, the need until the explosion began to grow from the hidden place within and find its culmination in every pore and every place in my body. *Ohh, yes.*

My back was against the door as I heard another toilet flush, the water run, a few words between women who had entered the bathroom before or after me. I turned and sat on the toilet, pretending I was doing what most people do when they're in the cubicle, making sure my feet were facing the right way in case anyone wondered, catching my breath and enjoying the last quivering of my clitoris. Then I stood, flushed the toilet, tidied my clothing with my hands, and walked out the door as if I had just relieved myself. In a certain sense, I had. I could either engage in secret bathroom masturbation or have sex with every Tom, Dick, or Harry who caught my fancy. Usually, I chose the first option. Little did I know I was a sexual creature until Sylvia came on the scene, and then all hell, or maybe heaven, broke loose.

As a young wife and mother, all my sexuality had been channeled into nursing my babies, raising my children, and satisfying my husband. Before that, I had little conscious experience with sex and, coupled with my extreme shyness, mostly avoided sexual expression. Even my procreative functions had been compromised by my sexual secrets. While giving birth to Lizzy, my traumatized vagina, vulva, and cervix would not relax to allow her to pass easily through the birth canal, which ultimately sent me into shock and close to death. Never had my sexuality felt like a natural part of my being, nor did I know how to use it playfully and with confidence. Instead, sexuality carried a sort of shame.

Sylvia changed all that. She burst forth, namelessly, on the scene not long after John and I separated, most certainly a subliminal response to the shock of his affair. While I saw myself as damaged goods, she saw me as beautiful, desirable, sexy even. She demonstrated—to my surprise—that she was good at sex. Sex, she found, gave me power. Men liked me because they liked sex. For a broken woman who felt powerless most of the time, sex in and of itself became seductive.

But Sylvia, who announced her name several years later in my journal, was more than raw sex. She embodied all my life-giving impulses. In the midst of my deepest despair, her moments of playfulness seemed to reside in my whole body, including but not limited to my genitalia. When I was depressed, Sylvia found joy simply by smiling and using facial response and body language to convey delight, interest, or curiosity to people regardless of their gender. Loving the outdoors and reveling in sun, shade, rain, flora, fauna, and the breeze that tickled her skin, she owned both my sexuality and my sensuality.

"I'm going to throw a party," said Sylvia aloud when my forty-fifth birthday rolled around. *Everyone else in this system is depressed or exhausted, including you,* she confided in me privately. *We have to have some fun!* She went about contacting friends from my local area as well as friends I had met in the women's unit.

On a sunny summer day in July, twelve women showed up in the backyard of my apartment. Everyone brought food, and Sylvia ordered a big, beautiful cake. Candida, the sister I had met in the unit, brought her guitar and played folk songs. We sat on the lawn or on folding chairs in the green space in the city, talking and laughing and renewing friendships. A big maple tree provided shade, and birds flew from tree to bush and back again, pecking at seeds hidden amid the foliage. My insides smiled. Every part of me, including the parts I didn't yet know, was overjoyed. Sylvia lifted us up when we couldn't do it ourselves.

In some ways, Sylvia was a lifesaver. When I was the most exhausted and discouraged, she took us dancing. When I thought the least of myself, she flirted her way into someone's heart. Sylvia was a teenager who hadn't yet learned how to control her desire, and her sexuality brought me close to danger on several occasions. But her joie de vivre was a much-needed contribution to my overall state of mind. When your inner life is chaos, your emotions a jumble, and you've flirted with suicide, having a part of you who can leave all that behind and have fun is nothing less than a miracle.

I began to teach Sylvia what she could and could not do. Bathroom masturbation was a bit disconcerting for me, but better than going on the prowl with real men who could be dangerous. Eventually, the intense need for non-contextual sexual release subsided, and I was able to explore sexuality within the context of healthy relationships. It was all about learning limits. Sylvia was an able learner and became a teacher herself. I taught her how to stay safe, and she taught me how to discover joy in the simple things—not without some complaining, I might add.

There's no time for any of us while you are teaching this college class, Sylvia groused one evening after a long day with first graders, an evening with college students, and late-night preparations for the next day. *Only Paula and a little bit of Laura get to do anything. Nanny incapacitates us, and Survivor picks up the ball, but I don't get to do anything. There's no fun anymore. No life. This college class is too much.* She remembered Debbie from the women's unit, who had taught her feminine things, fondly. *I don't even have time to paint my fingernails.*

One Saturday evening, I had an extended discussion among insiders regarding whether we should stay home and roll up into a ball or go to a local dance. There was some real wrestling among the troops: *I'm exhausted and need to rest. I've got too much to do and need to be responsible. I feel like a zombie and want to roll up in a ball.* But Sylvia won. *Sylvia lives!* I rejoiced. *Sometimes I think she is the only one inside who lives. We're going dancing tonight!* (8:00 pm) *I did it! I went and danced and had fun. I met John* (an old friend) *and came home and I'm safe.* ☺ *I lived!* (11:00 pm)

⌒

I began to have difficulties with the Quaker peace testimony. *Meeting for worship was difficult for me today,* I wrote in my journal. *People spoke of peace, of the "meek inheriting the earth." It feels to me that*

*there is hypocrisy or ignorance or innocence in peace without knowing
how to achieve peace. I don't want to be meek—I want to be strong. I am
having <u>great</u> trouble with the peace testimony.*

At the same time, I was deeply drawn to the peace testimony. Since
Quakers believe there is "that of God" in every person, how we manage
conflict rests on that foundation. If each person has a little piece of
God in him or her, then we have to respect them even if we don't agree
with them. We have to protect them even if we don't like them. We
have to find solutions to our disagreements, even when there appears
to be no path to reconciliation.

As a teacher, I was adept at helping children resolve their issues,
value each other, and learn skills to bridge differences. I taught respect
and kindness even under trying circumstances. My colleagues and
peers saw me as a peace-loving educator who brought that perspective
into both my personal and professional life.

Yet the further I went into my therapy, the more difficult it was for
me to reconcile the peace testimony with the perspectives of my alters,
especially Mike. His rage worked against any simplistic understanding
of peace. He was not about to lay down his anger for some pie-in-the-
sky religious belief.

*It's all well and good to talk about peace, but maybe that's for goody
two-shoes. What about when someone is hurting you? I'm not about to sit
there and take it. We've done that far too many times. We're going to stand
up now and fight for ourselves. We're not pacifists. If necessary, we'll fight to
the death!* To complicate matters, Mike and other alters began to have
fantasies about hurting or even killing their perpetrators. I couldn't be
much of a Quaker if I embraced those images. The whole of me still
believed that peace was the ultimate expression of God, but clearly my
system had ambivalent thoughts about what that meant to me.

⌒

Sylvia's sexual acting out is called *reenactment.* When a person
experiences trauma without processing it or taking steps to heal it, she

will reenact the trauma in her adult life until it is brought out of her unconsciousness into the light. Sylvia's love of life was authentic and healthy, but her reenactment was not. Using sex as power was a way to express her experience that sex had been used as power over her. Engaging in risky sexual behavior mimicked the extreme risk she had been exposed to as a young child. I had to teach her healthy context for sex at the same time I embraced her happy energy.

Once I asked Sonia, "Why would anyone want a man in their life?"

She surprised me by saying, "For companionship, being loved, and being known."

Hmmm, thought Sylvia. *That puts a whole new slant on relationship possibilities. I've never thought about companionship before. I'm not sure what being loved means. Being known sounds intriguing. Sex isn't even in the mix. Wow. I don't want to ditch sex, but I'll think about the other reasons for relationships too. I trust Sonia a little bit, and maybe she's onto something.* Sylvia embraced Sonia's answer easily. She was willing to let go of the exploitation pattern and try out this new paradigm.

Rosie also engaged in reenactment. I/she trusted too easily. It was not a mature trust but one that was based on her experience of climbing into "his" lap, getting hurt, then going back to trust again, and getting hurt again. She reenacted this pattern over and over as I presented with faux trust when I really didn't trust at all.

"I don't know what I'm going to do with them," Karen sighed as we sat in her first-grade classroom next to mine one afternoon after school. We were talking about her young-adult children, who were struggling to find their way into adulthood. Karen was older than me and way more experienced as a first-grade teacher. Traditional in her teaching approach, she was warm and loving to her students. I had noticed over the past year that she lacked confidence in her family life. Her self-doubt gave me a false sense of faith that she would hold anything I said in confidence. Some part of me needed someone I could confide in at school. Warm and loving? Self-doubt like me? Maybe this was someone I could trust.

"I know what you mean," I said. "I've been struggling too. Last year I was diagnosed with multiple personalities, and that's added a whole new dimension to my relationships with my kids." She looked at me in surprise and a little bit of compassion.

"Ooooh, that must be hard. I'm sorry to hear that," she replied. We didn't delve any deeper into my story, but I felt both relief and fear for having come clean with someone I worked with. Relief that I finally shared truthfully with another person. Fear that I shared too much and would get in trouble.

Sure enough, the next week I found a note in my school mail slot from Jill, my principal, asking to meet with me during my planning period. I sat in her finely appointed office, waiting for the other shoe to drop. The pit in my stomach grew. The icicles in my mind were already swaying, and I could barely remember where I was. Tall and glamorous, Jill swept into the room and took her place behind her massive walnut desk. She smiled at me with the assurance of a powerful administrator. I was quiet but quaking inside.

"I've been told that you have a diagnosis of multiple personality disorder. Is that true?" *You gave away the secret. How stupid could you be?*

"Yes, it is true. I'm in therapy now to work on the issues it brings up." We talked about my situation, and she revealed that she had discussed it with the assistant superintendent.

"I've talked with HR and they're aware of your situation." I was terrified and berating myself before I left her office. *You've put our whole system in jeopardy.* My condition was known not only by Karen, the teacher next door, and by Jill, my principal, but by the second-highest administrator in the district. *Who knows how many people are aware of the teacher who is crazy?* Parts of me were horrified and parts of me were enraged. *What made you think you could trust anybody with this information?* Jill was not unkind, but she responded from a position of responsibility, expecting me to inform her if my condition interfered with my teaching. *Only a weakling wants a confidant. You are a weakling.* "We have to deal with the hand we've been dealt," Jill concluded.

I left her office feeble with fear, consumed by inner backlash, which was common whenever I did something right but risky. *I've told. Now others know.* My knees were shaking. *I will get hurt.* My heart fell into my stomach, and my mind went into overdrive with castigation. *I will be fired. How stupid could you be?* I called Sonia as soon as I got home and poured the story out to her. *I'm going to die.* I journaled constantly over the next several weeks, berating myself for my stupidity. *Help me. Please.*

In the end, nothing bad happened as a result of my careless placement of trust, but I learned a hard lesson. Rosie's reenactment prevented me from assessing the drawbacks of disclosing. I began to see why I had trusted John even when the evidence of his infidelity was staring me in the face. A venereal disease early in our marriage. A plea for divorce, withdrawn as quickly as it was given. A confession of "almost" having sex with a Spanish woman met at a bar. With both John and Karen, I thought I trusted them, but my trust was a stand-in for need. Need drove my reenactments, not trust. I didn't authentically trust anyone.

CHAPTER 10

THE RING AROUND ROSIE

During my years of psychotherapy, Sonia moved her office twice. In both cases, it was within ten minutes of my apartment and convenient for me to access. The second move happened quickly and without much notice. I drove up to the complex, got out of the car, walked through the front doors, found the therapy room, and sat in an unfamiliar chair with a chip on my shoulder.

"Hello, Lyn. How are you?"

Silence.

How could she make such a big decision without realizing how it would affect me?

Silence.

"I'd like to hear what your week was like."

Silence.

It isn't safe here. It's not my space. She's mean and awful.

Silence.

I don't know where I am. I don't know what to do.

Silence.

It is a nice space and I can understand why she likes it. But, really, how could she?

Silence.

I hate her, I hate her, I hate her.

Silence.

Because Sonia was pretty nondirective in her approach, we sat there for eighty minutes in silence. Didn't she know it wasn't safe for me to tell her what I thought? Didn't she know I wasn't allowed to get angry with her, or anyone? Didn't she know I was trapped in a space I couldn't get out of and it was terrifying? My body writhed in fear, but I was stuck in a comfortable chair in a beautiful new office that wasn't safe.

Sonia didn't poke and prod to get me to talk. I have no idea what she was thinking, but she sat in her chair, looking at me with kindness and patience. At the end of the session, I got up and managed to say, "Well, that's it," and left the office with no promise I'd return next week. In the meantime, other voices inside were kicking me, saying, *We had things to talk about. Why did you waste that precious time? What were you thinking of?!*

Back home, I became unstuck and returned the next week without any fear of the new space, which over time became a womb where I could safely discover myself.

But for one session, someone inside needed to express the fear in a silent, excruciating hour and a half.

⁓

Laura was the part of me who gave birth to my children, raised them, and loved them. I had gotten pregnant two months after John and I married, an uneventful pregnancy but a traumatic delivery that brought me close to death. Yet Lizzy emerged alive and well with forceps marks around her temples.

Unbeknownst to me, the birth canal that had pushed Lizzy into the world also pushed forward the mothering me whose name I would later learn was Laura. I was co-conscious and had no idea that Laura was a separate part of me. She was alive and vivacious in the early years of my marriage, loving her children, loving her husband, loving her life. I/she discovered deep wells of love that I never knew existed when I mothered my children. I/she felt complete in the easygoing affection our family shared back and forth in our lives together. I/she identified as an effective and fulfilled mom who provided a nurturing environment for my children and a happy place for my family.

"Come here, all you little goofballs," I had called out to Lizzy and Kimmy from under my big warm quilt when they were preschoolers. We cuddled until everyone was exhausted with giggles.

"How about I make my fantastic carne molida for dinner after we have an afternoon quickie?" I had whispered into John's ear when the kids were playing outdoors and we had a minute or two to ourselves.

"Let's make cookies together." I had rescued Chuckie from the television set and another episode of *Sesame Street*. He scrambled up to the counter, and we became chefs supreme while the older kids were engaged in their own interests. These actions were all expressions of the Laura who was me, who loved her husband and her children.

Other than her initial introduction in my journal, Laura never spoke to me. I knew Laura existed separate from me mainly by her absence. She abandoned our family to protect herself from both internal and external danger. Her/my outer veneer had begun to peel away during student teaching, leaving her vulnerable and frightened. Her/my growing children's needs were more complex, confounding her simple approach to loving babies and toddlers. Her/my husband seemed distant and unapproachable, setting off internal alarms. The mood swings of the other parts she shared headspace with made the idyllic life of a loving mother increasingly elusive. Laura wasn't sure what this meant, but in her mind, it foretold a coming doom. She didn't disappear entirely and made appearances in the classroom on a regular basis. But her infidelity to my children was heartbreaking.

I had long given up on Laura returning home, but I implored her to reappear in the classroom after a stretch of low energy with my students had prevented me from teaching with heart. *I'm so tired I could drop*, I wrote in my journal. *I've finished my work and I'm in bed, but I want to write to say this. I feel so scared that I don't know who I am. That person who teaches the kids and loves my children so much is the person I thought was me. That was my identity as an adult for so many years. I lost that person, or that feeling. It has been scary and depressing to lose the me I know, identify with, respect, and love. But I did. I couldn't explain it and I still can't, but maybe I can a little bit now.*

Paula, on the other hand, felt no such angst. She was the professional part of me who was connected to Laura in some unconscious way; they were partners and worked together to make my life more effective. Paula seemed devoid of feelings and expressed them only when colluding with other alters in the system who had ample feelings to share. Her power was her fine mind, her critical thinking, and her professional ambition. While Laura was happy sitting on the floor with kids, Paula hobnobbed with teachers, parents, administrators, and experts in the field.

Of course you can create a Good Value Store here in public school, just like you did at the Quaker school, said Paula in my mind. I had been thinking about replicating it in my new classroom but was afraid I couldn't pull it off with the larger number of students. *Just because you have twice as many children in one classroom doesn't mean it won't work. In fact, it may work even better. I'll figure out the logistics and get in touch with the parents. I'll check in with the principal too. Laura, you can work with the children because that's what you do best. Nanny, it's best for you to stay home with Rosie and stay out of the way. Lyn, you can be out front because that's who everyone expects. We'll invite all the other first-grade classrooms to attend. It will be a great learning experience and a lot of fun for everyone.* With her usual competence and organizational skills, Paula hosted, collaboratively with me and other alters, an event that created a buzz in the whole school.

Paula had some magical way of transforming my other alters when they joined together in the classroom. When Paula attached to Laura, I could take a happy game with children and turn it into a top-notch curriculum goal. When she merged with Sylvia, I was the powerful, alive teacher who was the ultimate professional. When she merged with Laura, I was the sensitive, responsive teacher who loved children. When Paula merged with Laura and Sylvia together, I was at my best with my students.

I was proud of Paula's accomplishments and, by proxy, proud of myself.

Sadly, there were no negotiated partnerships in my home life where it seemed the danger to Laura had been initiated. With Laura gone, I was alone in parenting while Rosie was crying, Nanny was exhausted, Mike was fighting to move me forward, Sylvia was dying to go dancing, others were doing their own thing, and I had no idea these parts of me even existed. I just thought I was crazy. Laura may have carried the love for my children, but she was a part of me, and I loved them too, even if without feeling. With her gone, I had to relearn, over time, how to feel love, and I barely know how to put that process into words. I just went through the motions until the feelings eventually reappeared.

It was late September, and I was leading a parent night for my first-grade class. The walls of the classroom beamed with color, first attempts at writing, and other proud products of first-grade children. Everything started out great as I spoke animatedly to the parents. Laura, who commanded the classroom and related so well to children, began.

"I love teaching first-grade children. They are filled with wonder and awe and so ready to learn how to navigate learning."

"My son has a behavioral problem. How are you going to handle that?" asked one mother whose child occasionally acted out.

"Don't worry. Every child has unique challenges, and I'll call in a specialist if we need to. Usually, we have so much fun in the classroom that children naturally want to be part of the group. Even when they're naughty, I love them, and with luck, they come around."

As Laura continued talking, she dropped back, maybe due to the reference to behavioral problems that always seemed to confound her. Rosie, who was terrified to be in the middle of all those strange adults, was pushed to the front. *What's happening? Who are all these people? I'm afraid.*

I turned my back to cover my yawn, and Nanny jumped in to help. *Go back to sleep, Rosie. You're okay.* "I don't remember where we were.

Oh, yes, do you have any questions?" Nanny asked the parents. More fogginess, fading in and out. Nanny tried to field questions about the classroom she had no firsthand knowledge of at the same time she was comforting Rosie to keep her from sobbing in front of all the grown-ups.

"Yes, the children will be in writer's workshop four days a week and math workshop once a week." Rocking Rosie.

"They'll be working on little research projects appropriate for their reading ability, using the books you see in the corner." Holding Rosie close.

"I try to make their learning as experiential and hands-on as possible." *It will be over soon.*

When the last parent left, I sat on a teeny first-grade chair and stared into space, caught in a cognitive crunch that almost derailed my livelihood. Out of necessity, I had pushed through the icicles all evening, but now they shimmered not just in my mind but in every pore of my being. I never learned what happened to Laura. Paula, the professional who usually managed situations like these, was nowhere to be seen. Through my eyes, everything had been a blur, including the artwork on the walls. Looking back on it later, I realized I had no idea what I was saying before I said it. It just came spilling out like vomit from a sick child. Somehow, I managed to make it through the evening, but I had little memory of what happened and no control over it.

This incident jarred me to my core. Having insiders or alters was no game. If I didn't develop communication with them and set ground rules, the potential damage to my professional life was huge. It was a conundrum I was still figuring out: I seemed to have no choice but to give them a voice since they were grabbing the microphone with or without my permission. Yet somehow, I had to teach them when and how to speak, who could speak in what situations, and how they could work with each other to prevent situations like this from happening again.

In other words, I had to parent myself.

My parents named me Emlyn, an original name derived from my aunt whose name was Emily. They called me Lynn.

"Lynn, wake up, it's time for school."

"Lynn, make your bed before you go out to play."

"Lynn, watch your brother while I make dinner."

I used that spelling until I was in my late twenties when I dropped the final *n*. My husband, John, was changing a letter in his last name, so I thought it was as good a time as any to change the spelling of my first name. Who knows why I wanted a different spelling—maybe it was a belated effort to differentiate from my parents. Before my world started to fall apart, I still felt very close to them.

As it turned out, a small part of me kept my original spelling and stayed firmly rooted in the childhood I thought I had lived. Little Lynn was the good girl who never disobeyed her parents, never caused any trouble, and always thought her parents loved her. She proved to be very resistant to therapy and any suggestion that her parents were anything but good. When other alters revealed information, she stomped her foot and said, *It's not true.* She worried that I was starting to be an independent thinker and afraid that we would get into big trouble. As with Laura, I often thought I was Lynn and had difficulty distinguishing between myself and the good little girl because I had identified with her for much of my life.

My father used to hold Little Lynn in his lap and tickle me/her. He would laugh while reciting a jingle that was as much a threat as a game. "There was a little girl who had a little curl right in the middle of her forehead. When she was good, she was very very good, but when she was bad she was horrid." Then his fingers would quiver around my/her flesh to find the vulnerable places, and I would laugh too. I/Lynn knew I didn't want to be horrid because there would be consequences. Instead, I was good, very good.

As I drove home from a therapy session, the heat of the summer evening brought sweat to my forehead. My air conditioner was broken, so I had the windows rolled down. Antsy from my work with Sonia, I was tapping my fingers on the steering wheel. The old jingle began replaying in my head:

> *Ring around the rosies,*
> *Pocket full of posies,*
> *Ashes, ashes,*
> *We all fall down.*

Over the past weeks, I had begun to draw diagrams that showed how I thought my inner parts were connected to each other on any given day. Rosie and Nanny were a central part of the diagrams. So were Survivor, Little Lynn, Mike, Sylvia, Paula, and Laura.

In the first diagram, Rosie was in the middle with Nanny, Sylvia, Little Lynn, Laura, Paula, and Survivor radiating from her center. Broken lines to Lynn, Laura/Paula, and Survivor indicated they didn't know Rosie existed. My notes said, *When I was a little schoolgirl, Lynn was dominant. When I was raising little children, Laura was dominant. Now, Rosie is dominant, but everyone is popping up.*

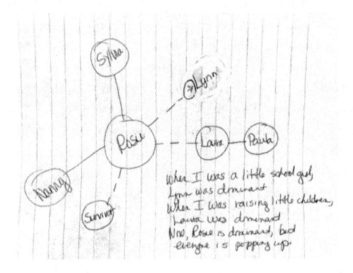

The second diagram showed Rosie in the middle with Survivor, Lynn, Sylvia, and Nanny growing out of Rosie, and Nanny in a triangle with Laura and Paula, who didn't know Rosie or Nanny existed. I was taking baby steps to understand my system: who they were, what they knew, how they interacted with each other.

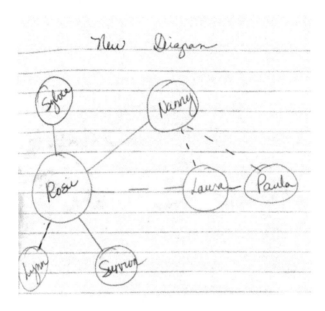

When Mike came on the scene shortly after Sylvia, my diagram changed yet again. In the third diagram, Rosie remained firmly in the middle, radiating Mike, Sylvia, and Nanny, all of whom knew about Rosie and existed in some sense to protect her. Laura was also one of Rosie's rays but didn't know she existed; nor did Paula know about Rosie at the time this diagram was created. Paula emerged from Laura and, eventually, became aware of all my parts as my amnesic walls lowered. Paula knew about Nanny because of intense arguments between them— Paula was the finely tuned professional who left Nanny in the dust to take care of Rosie. Little Lynn was unaware of Rosie and, in some sense, was the child in competition with Rosie for the narrative of what our childhood was like. In this diagram, I noted not only the parts who were conscious of Rosie and who were not, but I also noted with dark circles who "I identified myself with at some time in my life." With time and therapy, all my parts came to know and cooperate with one another, but that was not the case at the outset.

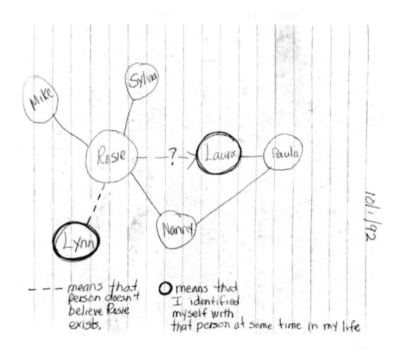

Everyone seemed to have their own ideas about how I should manage my life. Mike and Sylvia, especially, had strong opinions that sometimes shook things up. Teenagers who were twins and two sides of the anger–sexuality coin, they lacked self-discipline. Occasionally, they stormed off and took matters into their own hands.

I'm pissed off that you're acting like a victim. I'm going to do what I want to do, Mike would tell Little Lynn when she refused to speak directly to a school administrator. *I'm going to talk to him even if you're afraid.*

Oh, I'm sooooo tired of sitting around here doing nothing, Sylvia would moan when Rosie wanted to crawl under the covers and cuddle with our stuffed animals. *I'm going to a dance, have a drink, and flirt, whether you want to or not.*

Usually, I called a family meeting to resolve disagreements, but they weren't always successful. *I felt sick to my stomach all day today,* I wrote in my journal. *Tried to have a family meeting, but everybody wanted to walk out. Some insiders think other insiders are wimps, no fun, not worth hanging around to talk with. I said maybe we can come back later when we calm down a bit and talk. I slept for a half hour outside. Feel a little better. I am scared. Nanny is scared. Nanny knows why. I don't.* Mostly, though, my system was relatively peaceful. We drew on our experience with Quaker consensus to give everyone a chance to talk and share their opinions.

I was thinking about all this while I stopped at McDonald's and ordered a Big Mac and a giant Diet Coke. The sun was setting as I drove back to my apartment, eating my fast-food dinner in the car. I sipped the ice-cold drink slowly to keep me hydrated. It had been a long day and I was tired. Really, I just wanted to get home in time to watch another episode of my favorite sitcom, but my journal diagrams had given me a lot to think about. I had met the foundational personalities in my system. I was beginning to understand the role each of them played, what they knew and didn't know, and how they got along with each other. I parked my car under the large maple tree in the back of my building and just sat there.

Who am I, literally? I asked myself. *There is no Lyn—after all, my given name was Emlyn, I used the nickname Lynn as a child, and I changed the spelling as an adult. Alters pick up so much of my functioning that I, as an entity, seem irrelevant.* These questions were existential.

As the diagrams grew, I realized they all had Rosie in the middle. There was always a ring around Rosie. Protector chimed in, *There is a rhyme or reason, Lyn. I created your system. Then I taught you to sing "Ring Around the Rosie."*

CHAPTER 11

PAIN

*T*hrobbing, I wrote in my journal. *Breathing. Breathing isn't easy. It's a commitment. I don't like commitments. Sometimes, it's hard to breathe.* Thousands of pages tumbled out, at least half of which were scribbles about unbearable pain, unfathomable hate, unthinkable suffering, and the inexorable movement toward death. *I am so afraid. When I am afraid, I can't move. I want to crawl into a corner and die. I will be hurt. People hurt me. I don't know why they hurt me, but they always do. Sometimes when they hurt me it just feels bad; sometimes I know I will die.*

From the years before I was diagnosed through my ten years of deep therapy, and even in some years beyond my recovery, pain— physical, emotional, and psychic pain—was a constant companion. Every moment of every day was a battle to maintain my sanity in the presence of pain that seemed to have no source. Each molecule of my skin throbbed with the history of the hidden memories in residence in my body. Without a narrative, my flesh had no reason for living or context for dying. Beneath was an inexplicable terror that I was responsible for my own demise and the destruction of everyone and everything I loved. Within the pummeled shell of pain was the shame of simply being, existing, living—death would be so much more sensible than living. Nausea sometimes accompanied me when an alter came forward or a memory peeked around the corner. Breath was hard. Suicide was always an option.

*I am sinking fast. If I'm not careful, it will eat me up. It will consume me. Right now, I want to die. I don't want to live. The pain is too lousy. I don't even want to **want to** live. I don't want to know how. I just want to end it.*

~

When Sonia talked, some part of my mind listened. Carefully. To every syllable. To meaning. And nuance. And undertone. *She said this, but did she mean that? She tells you that, but is it really this?* Once Snake introduced himself in my journal and in the therapy room, I recognized his nameless but menacing gaze from past therapy sessions.

Snake was visceral, cunning, and sly. I felt his long, slender body glide over every word Sonia spoke, taking in the agenda he believed was hiding under every rock, slithering beneath, above, and through the twists and turns of prefixes, suffixes, endings, and other word parts that changed the meaning of a sentence. If alters were going to reveal hidden truths, Sonia's motivation had to be thoroughly dissected. When you lived among mindfuckers, words were weapons. Snake used his body as a sensor, and the information he took in were the subtleties of Sonia's words, her tone, her eyes, and the underbelly of her being. Each time he was satisfied with the data he had collected, he would glide away as quickly as he appeared.

You are of no interest to me, Snake sniped, speaking with piercing eyes I couldn't see but could feel slinking in and out of the organs in my body. Intense, rage-filled, and a coil of shame, he claimed to have been created in the moment of the first penetration and imagined he fled the body to escape the searing pain of rape. Never revealing the details of his sinister creation, he tormented me with aggressive swipes instead. *You are inconsequential. Irrelevant. Your body may have been convenient, but it's of no worth to me.* He was spirit, or so he said, hissing his way into and out of my consciousness. My death would be just fine with him because he was sure he would continue to live on in his out-of-body existence.

I don't need that body. Just a limp excuse for a body. Just a body that can be hurt. My rage can live outside this body. If the body dies, I will still live. I will always live. I will crawl between the cracks and kill the fucking son of a bitch. He can take the body, but I will still live. In his world beyond care or connection, he was responsible for both suicidal and homicidal ideation. *I live on his pain. It feeds me. I will never die, just so I can feed on him. Someday his eyes, his skin, his entrails, his blood will cry out, and I will laugh and settle down and digest my feast.* My body shivered as Snake wound through the convolutions in my mind, turning pain into a plan of action.

"Sonia, this is awful. How can I live with such a cruel part of me talking in such terrible ways?" I cried, stunned and nauseated as his words moved slowly forward to obliterate the me I thought I was. Sonia received Snake in the same way she received all of my alters—with graciousness.

"Welcome. I'm so glad you're here. I hope you'll come back often. You're safe now."

I was a sun worshiper who loved to sit outdoors in my lounge chair where the sun baked away the traces of my psychic scars. I found that Snake, too, sat on rocks in the sun to soak up the solar energy that fueled his existence. In an unexpected act of allegiance, he professed his protection to Lizzy, Kimmy, and Chuck. *They are sacred,* he whispered like a dark lord casting shadows on the walls of an ancient tunnel. *They cannot be touched. You fucking bastard. Stay away from them,* he warned. *They are pure and good. They are God's light. They are beautiful. No matter what they do, they have purity and white light inside.* Then he took the oath of fealty. *I will protect them. My rage wraps around them. I will not hurt them,* he declared as if convincing himself. *I will not. I will rip out your eyes if you touch them,* he closed with the threat gliding through fangs ready to pierce the flesh of anyone who disobeyed him.

Snake's devotion to my children was the fire in the pit of my belly that raged against whatever caused them pain. I didn't seem to be able to impact their emotional health myself, so Snake held my venom that would immobilize anyone or anything that would harm them. Snake would defend what I could not.

Although Snake's opinion of Sonia varied by his data crunch on any given day, he warmed to her suggestion that he might be a hurt child. When she treated him with respect, his rage dissipated, though it never fully went away in order to keep watch over my real children and to rout out the mindfuckers in my midst.

≈⟩

I had been praying for a nice man to come into my life. *It doesn't have to be the man I will spend the rest of my life with, God. I just want a good man who I can do things with. I need to have a little fun.* As much as I wanted to meet the love of my life, I knew I wasn't healthy enough to attract the kind of man I would want to marry someday. A good friend would have to do until I was ready for more. I dated several men I had met at events I attended; each one of them had good points, but I knew none of them would become a life partner. Some, though, became fellow travelers on my healing journey.

"May I have this dance?" asked a nice, red-haired man at the social center in the city. Rod was a great dancer, like me, so we really lit up the dance floor. When a waltz came on, he charmed me with the strong way he held me and led me across the floor without a trip or misstep. He paid a lot of attention to me, and I was flattered. "Could I take you to dinner tomorrow night?"

"Yes, that would be lovely," I said, thinking, *Finally, here is a nice man I could have fun with.* It turned out he was a minister who was getting a divorce, and I was a new Christian who had already been through a divorce, so we had a lot in common. We served as mentors and healing guides for each other. It was never meant to be a romance, but we remained friends for many years.

I met Chris at Bethlehem's Musikfest one summer night. We were both standing up against a food kiosk and listening to a folk group. The summer breeze was welcoming. "What other kind of music do you like?" he asked, munching on a bag of french fries.

"Oh, there isn't much music here I don't like," I said, thinking of the pop, jazz, reggae, polka, classical, and more that was all around me in every crevice of the city. All I had to do was walk outside my front door for ten days in August to hear a whole potpourri of musical genres.

"Let's try Americaplatz tomorrow night," he suggested. He offered me a fry.

"Sounds like a good idea," I accepted and popped the hot, crunchy morsel into my mouth. Chris was the first corporate type I had dated, and he unearthed an explosion of fear among my insiders I hadn't experienced with the other men on my dance card. I spent hours writing pros and cons, developing charts, and weighing the merits of seeing him, having sex with him, being vulnerable with him. As much as Sylvia enjoyed her time with Chris, the rest of my system was in crisis mode. *He's totally un-self-aware. You don't want to go into a relationship with someone like that. He's cute and he pays attention to me. All he wants is sex and watching football games. Give him a chance. We hardly know him. Your values aren't the same. Oh, pooh. Who cares? He's an IRS agent, for God's sake. He's too much like John. DON'T do it.* Without warning, after the first and only time I had sex with him, a part of me came out and ended it.

I called him. "I'm sorry, Chris. You're a nice man, but I don't think I can see you again."

"Why not? I thought we were getting along great."

"I don't know. It just doesn't feel right. Good luck." And I hung up the phone.

The Black Knight, I learned, chopped off people's heads. He chopped off Chris's head. He chopped off the heads of other friends who tried to get intimate. He chopped off job possibilities, opportunities, and more. Although I didn't know it at the time, his motivation was to protect me from people and situations he thought were dangerous. At the root, he acted out of fear. The Black Knight wasn't a constant actor in my inner drama, but, when needed, he rode his white steed into the fray and chopped someone's head off, swift and fast. *It's over. Thank you very much, but goodbye.* The Black Knight to the rescue.

His poetic proclivities were as dramatic as his actions:

Here I am.
The Black Knight escapes.
The Princess is dangling.
I am hopeless, helpless.
The wall still stands.
But I breathe.
And the baby waits.
And the river torrents on like blood through my veins.

I never fully understood what this theatrical flourish meant, but I did know that the Black Knight's need to vanquish potential danger was a well-meant but unhealthy attempt to keep me safe.

I taught first grade for two years at the premier school in the district yet felt somehow out of place. When I had the chance, I applied for and received a transfer to one of the neediest schools that serviced 60 percent second-language learners, children of diversity, and many of poverty. Two years later, the same school offered me a position with administrative duties and push-in support for teachers in the classroom. To accommodate my new load of paperwork, I had my own small office in a corner of the library. I continued to face exhaustion, confusion, conflicting inner messages, and something akin to panic attacks. All the while, I journaled daily, attended weekly individual and group therapy sessions, and tried to make it through one day at a time.

It took just over six years for John and me to agree on a property settlement. The process was grueling, and any sense of regret for the fantasy marriage that was no more was overshadowed by immense relief at putting the whole macabre experience behind me. With my small settlement, I paid off a few bills and bought a new box spring and mattress that seemed like luxury to me. Fourteen-year-old Chuck's grades had been suffering, so John invited him to live with Kimmy and him, certain that Chuck's apathy was related to my poor parenting. I lived in my two-bedroom apartment, alone.

Not long after, at the age of seventeen, Kimmy began to have difficulties with John's strict disciplinary parenting. It was not a good match for her sensitive nature. After a particularly difficult altercation between them, she asked to live with me, and I happily welcomed her into the same two-bedroom first-floor apartment in Bethlehem that Chuck and I had shared. Our life together wasn't roses either, and she entered her senior year of high school still troubled and prone to push hard against house rules. In the fall, she turned eighteen and took the initiative to drop out of school without my knowledge or consent. A few days later, she wrote me a note to tell me she loved me, then drove to her father's house.

I was in my office when John called. I heard him choke the words through the telephone receiver that a parent never wants to hear: "Kimmy attempted suicide. She's in the hospital here. Come quickly."

This can't be true, I screamed silently. *It didn't happen. It's not real.* After I hung up the phone, I stood in the middle of my four walls, looked up at the ceiling in an effort to see God somewhere beyond the bricks and mortar closing in on me, and cried out in rage, "God, I can't believe you're asking this from me, yet again. What else do you want? What more do you expect?"

The world wasn't real as I raced forward in slow motion. I put on my coat, *and the sun shining through the window was gray and cold.* I grabbed my purse, *and the teal-colored rug faded in and out.* I barged into the hallway, *and the sharp shine of the tile disappeared in my speed.* I stopped at the main office to tell the principal I had a family emergency, *and the massive glass doors reflected my fear.* I couldn't feel anything because I was afraid I would feel everything. I walked quickly out the door and drove madly to the hospital where I discovered she was going to be okay.

I exhaled deeply, and slowly let go of the horror that could have been. Then I had Kimmy transferred to the women's unit at Northwestern so she could have some of the same benefits I had reaped. She used that time to great advantage and began to do serious therapeutic work of her own. I told her how proud I was of her and how strong I thought she was. She looked at me in apparent disbelief, but it was true. I knew from my own work that facing the pain was half the battle; if she could face it, she could heal and move forward. Her willingness to feel her pain was a measure of her bravery.

Chuck had his own fish to fry. After Kimmy's brush with death, he began to express his unhappiness with morbid poetry, Goth art, and failing grades. He was still living with his dad, but his teacher called me in concern.

"Chuck, Mrs. White called me about your poetry and your Goth art," I said when he visited. We were sitting in his bedroom—the same one he had claimed when we first moved to Bethlehem and the same one his sister Kimmy had used. "She's afraid you're depressed and might harm yourself. Can we look at some of your creative work together?" I was terrified he would repeat what his two sisters had attempted. I would do whatever it took to prevent that.

"Mom, you don't need to worry about me," he reassured me after we read one of his poems and examined his art. He was gifted, but the subject matter raised red flags. "It's just the way I get my feelings out. I'm not going to hurt myself or anyone else."

I sensed he was being truthful. I spoke to his teacher and told her about our conversation. Then I called him several times a week to see how he was doing. His mood was stable, but I continued to watch his grades fall. So I researched private schools and found a local therapeutic high school. Pulling some strings in his school district, I managed to have him placed there for the remainder of tenth grade.

"How's it going, Chuck?" I asked on one of my phone calls to see how he was faring in his new school.

"I hate it."

"Oh, come on. It can't be that bad. How is it structured?"

"It's not structured."

"What kind of work do you do? Do they have therapeutic groups for you?"

"I told you, I hate it. We hardly do any work. We just sit around and do nothing," he said with a strange mixture of boredom and passion. It seems he hated it so much that he worked hard to be discharged to his regular high school for his junior year, which was our goal in the first place. It looked like the therapeutic high school had done the trick.

Back in his home high school, he majored in art where the creative urges that had fueled his Goth-related expressions were rechanneled into beautiful expressions in multiple art forms. Surprising all of us, every medium he picked up he excelled at. His art teachers said, "You only get a student like Chuck once or twice in your lifetime." He graduated a year later with an award for best artist in his class.

What could have been tragedies for both Kimmy and Chuck became Kimmy's deepening self-awareness and Chuck's self-expression through art. I was more than grateful that they were resilient in the face of their inner turmoil. The overwhelming love I felt for each of them was small comfort for their angst I was sure was my fault. I carried my grief heavily, balanced by a smidgeon of hope as their pain mixed with mine, then separated again, taking flight toward me and away from me, both at the same time.

CHAPTER 12

RAGE

I bounced into Sonia's office one Thursday afternoon, excited to tell her I had met a new friend. Maybe I would be able to trust this man. It was new ground and something to celebrate. She grinned broadly and said, "I knew you could do it. You're a very likable person." I basked in my happiness for a while and chatted with Sonia about inconsequential things.

As usual, my words eventually petered out, so I closed my eyes and drifted into silence. The vast expanse of nothingness crowded me out of my body, and I sat suspended in between the breaths I took in and the breaths I pushed out. Now and then I yawned. Again, silence. Again, nothingness. The throbbing underneath my skin advanced its way through my blood vessels into my extremities like an expedition into a treacherous wilderness until every portion of me joined the drumbeat of my heart. Breathing became shallow. In the darkness, I was on high alert. Again, voices crept out, slowly, carefully.

"*It's there,*" hissed Snake, removing himself from his sentry position in my brain. "*Where? I don't know but I can feel it. Down. There. I. Want. To. Fucking. Kill. You,*" he wheezed, telling his story of humiliation and degradation. Red explosion of color in my eyeballs. Rage and hate. "*The knife.*" Snake began to talk faster. "*Can I cut it off? Please?*" Searing pain. "*Too much blood . . . Ooh, it hurts very much*

. . . "The pain moved up my torso into every pore of my body. I sat in the blue therapy chair and listened to the words, but I didn't believe them. They were coming from my mouth, but they weren't coming from me. I took a deep breath and kept my eyes closed. Time was unimportant. I switched.

"*The arms. The arms,*" cried Little Lynn in a panic. It seemed she was talking about the same incident but reporting on it from her own vantage. "*I must be very bad.*" Discomfort. "*They are tied up around the wrists behind my back.*" Fear. "*That's where they are. Right there. And I can't move them very well.*" Disbelief. "*I can't move, but if I'm very good and quiet, then I'll be okay.*" Denial. "*I won't hurt, you won't hurt me, because I'm good.*" Immobility. "*Can't you see how good I am?*" Resistance. "*I'll just be quiet here. I won't yell or scream.*" Rage. "*Good girls just sit and are quiet and then nothing will happen to them. Because they are sooooo good . . .*"

I was breathing fast and rubbing my wrists while I spoke. I put my head in my hands and waited for whatever would or would not come next. Another switch. It was unusual for multiple alters to visit Sonia at a time.

"*Right, and nothing happens to Little Lynn because I take it,*" said Nanny. "*You disappear and I'm left. It hurts. You just don't know how much it hurts. You are too busy being good and disappearing.*" The switches came more quickly.

"*Fuck. Didn't you hear me saying to run away?*" asked Mike. "*Kick him. Bite him. Kill him.*"

"*Oh, no. I didn't hear anything,*" said Little Lynn. "*I just disappeared. I thought it was good to be good.*"

I settled back into my body as a soldier home from battle, wiped out, sweaty, shaken. Lifting my head and opening my eyes, I looked around the room and took in the rug on the floor, the paint on the walls, the nubby bumps on the ceiling. Then I turned my gaze to Sonia. She didn't look shocked, just concerned. Unlike me, who couldn't believe a word I had heard that afternoon, she believed every voice. "Why would they lie, Lyn?"

I didn't know why they'd lie, but I didn't even understand everything they were trying to communicate. It was cryptic but chilling. Penetrating pain. Ropes around my wrists. A knife. My whole body was raw and in pain. I tried to put the pieces that were revealed into a box, but they just sat there in the air and followed me home. Everything that happened that day resonated with me, but it didn't make sense. I barely made it into my bedroom to curl up to sleep by eight o'clock.

≋

I'm holding "his" hand. We are in the big, ugly city. I don't remember how we got here. We walk along the cement sidewalk, past old run-down stores, and into one where the window is so dirty I can't see through it. A lot of men are sitting around in folding chairs and straight chairs with torn stuffing. They look old and some have scrubby hair on their faces. I hold my red pocketbook over my shoulder and close to me. The men give "him" money, and he leaves me with them. I don't remember what happens after that.

≋

I've always had a conflicted relationship with money. When I divorced, John's relentless withholding of child support and small final settlement left me with very little to lean on. My inner chaos and John's rage were not a good mix for equitable negotiations.

The roots of my immobility seemed to grow out of my father's obsessive control over money. In spite of the fact that we lived close to poverty growing up, he had accumulated a nice nest egg by the end of his life. When he was losing power over me, he would try to lure me back with financial treats and threats about my inheritance. If I did what he wanted, he would cover this or help me with that. If I didn't do what he wanted, I would lose those small benefits and, more importantly, he would cut me out of his will.

"If you don't see fit to respond to your old man, then I have no other choice than to cut you out of my will," he told me in a brief note he sent to me several years after I'd been disowned. I came to terms with the situation inwardly, knowing my mental and emotional health were more important than any financial benefits. I was surprised many years later when, upon his and my mother's deaths, I learned he had left me half my portion of his estate. I hadn't expected anything. The other half of my portion went to John.

With my father still alive and our relationship estranged, I was teaching in the public school in Bethlehem. Although I made a lot more money than I had earned at the Quaker school, I was still barely making ends meet. I couldn't think of buying a house. I couldn't do the kinds of things for my children I would have liked to do. I was barely able to scrape up enough money for a sorely needed vacation.

I pondered other ways to increase my financial stability. *Maybe I should think about becoming a public-school principal*, I thought. *I'm a great leader and administrator, and I've already done this kind of work at the Quaker school. The pay is much better, and it would put me in a stronger position both financially and personally.* More than an ample paycheck, becoming a principal would allow me to play with the power that comes with leadership, although I didn't factor that into my decision at the time. Assuming leadership, I would find, was a way to heal my fear of power. If I could use power for good, maybe I could heal the terror I felt each time I came face-to-face with power in someone else.

That was that. Five years after I left the women's unit, I attended a state university to qualify for a school administrator's certificate and found myself easily hired by a local site-based school district at the age of forty-nine. I would remain in that role for five years, learn the public-school ropes, develop curriculum, and create a comprehensive in-service training program. Utilizing power fairly and for good purposes was stimulating and motivated me to grow in leadership. At the same time, it took a toll on my inner world, which was still fully invested in therapeutic healing. With the uncovering of many alters with their own unique perspectives, my desire to find the memories that would explain their existence grew dramatically. How could I heal if I didn't know what had happened to me? What were my insiders hiding from me? Did they themselves even know? Inner conversations between myself and my system abounded.

~

For years, a shadow of shame followed me wherever I went. If the difference between shame and guilt is "I am bad" versus "I did something bad," then my whole existence was grounded in shame. No matter how hard I tried to do good things, I was bad. I was worthless. I was useless. I was wrong. Little Lynn had made sure I was a good girl, but still this dark cloud haunted me constantly in spite of her efforts to clean me up and make me presentable.

I am very bad, said this shadow of shame who was always with me. *I am like tar and caked with thick, moist dirt. You can scrape it off me. I am so bad. I am bad because I am not right. I am wrong. That is why I have to be right. I can't be wrong,* said the cloud, using circular logic. *Because I don't want to be bad. And I don't want to be dirty.* For the longest time, the shadow remained an organ within my body without shape or form, pumping out dirt, ugliness, and shame into my whole being, much the way the heart pumps blood into the body.

Eventually, this dark cloud introduced himself to me as an alter whose name was the Devil. One day in therapy, the organ of shame began to speak, angry, hurting, hurling insults at Sonia. *"My name is the Devil and I'm mean and terrible. You'd better be afraid of me because I do bad things. I'm awful. I'm despicable. I hate you."*

"Devil, it's so nice to meet you."

"Why would you think it's nice to meet me? Who would be glad to meet me? That's why I stay hidden inside her. Because I'm disgusting and nobody wants to meet me. Stay away from me. I might hurt you. I hate you. I hate everybody. I'm so bad."

"Devil, I'm impressed you've come up and introduced yourself. That took a lot of courage. You must be very hurt and lonely in there by yourself. I'm glad you're here." Sonia continued her relentless welcoming of my alters even when they appeared mean and dangerous. Devil embodied the most degrading images of myself and spewed his shame into every corner of my existence. His poison was ready to shut my whole system down. Little by little, peeking through the shimmering icicles, the Devil revealed the trauma that created him through my voice.

"*Downstairs in my grandma's and grandpa's place, there was a long, dark room along the side of the apartment. This was before my Daddy had reorganized it for their living space,*" said the Devil in a small voice. "*I think it was a bedroom. There was a bed. People were all around the bed, but I don't know who they were. There was a body on the bed, and they made me climb on top of the body, take a knife, and kill the body. I didn't want to do it,*" the Devil cried. "*My hands were holding the knife. Someone took my hands in theirs and raised my arms over my head. With huge force, they pushed my arms down so the knife entered the body. There was blood everywhere. I cried. I was scared. I didn't want to do it, but I did,*" said the Devil with surreal calmness mixed with mounting anxiety. His voice was flat but shaky. My voice was flat but shaky. I sat in silence, one tear sliding down my cheek.

Did I kill someone? Was this true? It had to be a made-up story. While the Devil inside me remained flat in the telling, the rest of me began to panic. *I'm a murderer. I've killed someone. No wonder I think I'm bad, defective, horrible.*

"Lyn, you were too small to be able to murder someone with a knife. I believe your story, but I don't believe you murdered anyone. It was a maneuver to control you, to keep you under their power. You did not kill anyone."

I went home from that session and cried. I didn't believe the story the Devil recalled. I didn't believe anything remotely similar happened and thought it was all my imagination. I took heart in Sonia's reassurance that I never killed anyone, but unlike her, I didn't believe the scene had any connection to reality. The only thing I believed was the shame that continued to ooze out of my body like molten tar moving slowly over a surface, filling the cracks and covering all.

Still, the memory incapacitated me, and I curled into a catatonic stupor once again. *Does Sonia think I like feeling ugly and dirty? I don't want to come to the surface. I want to hide so I can't feel myself and you can't either. I want to disappear. Just keep me covered. Don't let anyone know I'm here.* We revisited the memory several times. I had a sense of who may have been there but never confirmation. The scene never changed. The long, dark room, the people gathered around, the body on the bed, the knife, the act, the blood. The details remained the same, but they never became more real. My visceral tuning fork vacillated from flat and silent to loud and dissonant. As with other memories, the back-brain fragments never crossed the bridge into a front-brain, believable narrative. The urge to discard the terrifying story was huge, so we worked with the Devil in my current-day real world, leaving the fairy tale intact for some other child, but not for me.

The Devil, as it turned out, was tiny like Rosie, her *dark-side alter*. After he shared his memory, he began to scream with more potency than the wails of a newborn baby. His shrieks pierced my body like a sword against flesh, distressing all my other insiders with his frantic anguish. In an effort to quiet him, Nanny covered his cries with a blanket of food. *I take care of the babies,* she said. *But the Devil is dirty and ugly, so why shouldn't I want to hide him? I'm exhausted and he's difficult to have around. When I eat, the food goes directly and organically into the Devil. It covers, smothers, and molds to his shape so I can't see or feel him. No one knows he's there. The food hides him. It has its purpose.* I sometimes struggled with weight gain and began to use this knowledge of how my system was using food to control the out-of-control sounds of shame to find other ways to calm the Devil.

Somehow, I know that if I do something very sweet and nice for the Devil, I won't have to eat. But I can't think of what. Something really sweet. Like a little song or a finger play. Oh my. He must be very, very young. Dancing too. Not Sylvia kind of dancing. Just moving my arms around. And smiling. Instead of eating.

Mike wanted my system to get healthy, so he intervened with

Nanny to help her soothe the Devil. Together, they rocked both the Devil and Rosie, held them as little twins, pushed them in a carriage, played with them, and calmed their infant needs. I discovered my role in caring for these little parts of me. *They need to have me take care of them. Protect them,* I wrote in my journal. *Be an adult for them and even hide them, if necessary, if they are frightened and scared. Stand up for them. That is so important to know. Now I know.*

While walking through the Moravian Book Shop in Bethlehem, I found a little pink stuffed pig named Rosie. I fell in love with her immediately and bought her as a stand-in for the real Rosie. Several months later, I saw a duplicate for sale, only this one was black like the Devil. What serendipity. I held those two little stuffed animals close to me much of the time, imagining I was loving and protecting them. At some point, I bought a larger, floppy bear who became Mike. The three stuffed animals, representing my hurt alters and their protector, became my constant companions. Nanny was appreciative of Mike's and my efforts to soothe the little ones and was able to take a much-needed break.

No Name was buried in a tunnel inside me, and no one knew he existed. I met him one night when I attended a journaling workshop. The topic we were to write about was a "Letter or Dialogue with Someone Who Is Unavailable." I had expected to begin writing about my father, but instead this new voice emerged on my page.

Ha. You wanted this letter to be to your father because you think he's unavailable. But I am here because I am the most unavailable to you. I hold the memories and I won't let them go. It's my job to protect them. I was given that job many years ago—who cares how many. It was forever ago, and it will always be my job.

Sometime before No Name appeared, I had a memory that I/Rosie was locked in a closet. *My wrists are tied with rope,* I/Rosie had written in my journal. *I feel the fiber rub against my skin. It leaves a sore spot. I don't know how to get out of the closet by myself. I am lost. I smell the mothballs in the pockets. I feel the scratch of a wool coat brush against my face. My back is curled up against this little space. It is dark when I close my eyes, and it is dark when I open them. I cry very quietly. Everyone is gone and I am alone.*

Eventually, someone came back and let me out, but I didn't know who put me in there or who let me out. No Name embodied Rosie's fear and abandonment that actually belonged to me while I was locked in the closet. Rosie and I both got out of the closet, but No Name had remained there all those years, living inside my body. For him, the closet became a long, dark tunnel with no way out. *No Name and others, afraid to be here. Alone. No one to help, to take care of me.*

Once No Name discovered there was a world outside the tunnel, he kept trying to make his way up and out of it. *I want to get out of this fucking tunnel,* he said. *I don't like it down here. It's awful. I didn't know there was a way out. Now I know there is fresh air, sunshine, raindrops. I want to be up there. Get me the fuck out.*

No Name was also responsible for the word *nothing* in my writing. Over and over, when I asked myself questions in my journal, the answer would come back tersely: Nothing.

It is so confusing to me. I knew what I was supposed to do and I did it well. I knew I was saving you, protecting you, doing what I needed to do so you could survive. Now everyone tells me I'm supposed to let the memories go. It doesn't make sense.

I have them here in this little box. See—right here. They are all right in here. What am I supposed to do with them? They will kill you. Even I don't know what they are. They are in this box. The lid is tight. That's enough for now. No name. Nothing.

By the time No Name came on the scene, I had learned how to advocate for my alters and soothe their fears. I parented No Name and assured him I was there. *Breathe in. Breathe out,* I told No Name, leading him through a guided meditation. *Breathe in God's love. God is always here. Breathe out the fear. You are not alone. Breathe in. Breathe out. Actually, I am here for you, No Name. I, Lyn, am here for you. I love you, and I can take care of you. Breathe in. Breathe out. You are not alone. You are not trapped.*

No Name was the last of my alters to integrate. He struggled with abandonment issues that I had mostly healed myself. I reassured him many times that I would never leave him, even if he did decide to integrate. One day he disappeared on his own, finally free from his dark existence, reveling in the fresh air, and presumably taking a box full of memories with him.

It was late at night and I couldn't sleep. Tossing and turning, I twisted my blankets into a ball. My mind was racing, and my body was nauseous. I felt sweat beads collect in the folds of my face. *I am in so much pain. But now I know enough to say, "I am dissociated." It's hard to move. The pain wants its turn. We've hidden it for too long. Hard to breathe. Want to sleep. Can't.* Turning on my bed lamp, I grabbed my robe and limped into the kitchen to make myself a cup of warm tea. I needed to settle. For the past month, my hips had been hurting for no apparent reason. The neighbors' lights were off, but the streetlights cast a warm glow on the parked cars. It was quiet.

In my pottery-kilned cup, the tea bag seeped peppermint into the hot water. I brought it back to my bed and sipped slowly, my journal by my side. I closed my eyes, breathing in and out. My racing mind released one thought after another until I settled into the nothingness I often felt in Sonia's office. Not sleep but not conscious awareness. In. Out. At first shallow. Then deeply. Darkness. Nothing. Me. I set my half-empty cup on my nightstand and reached for my journal. Words flowed through my fingers onto the paper, slowly at first, mindlessly, picking up the pace as the story unfolded.

Snake was curled up in Rosie's red pocketbook, the one her daddy had bought her when she was two years old. He loved to crawl up inside where it was dark, away from the rest of the world. I saw the strap, crossed over my body from hip to shoulder. Oh, how I loved that pocketbook. But not now. *The strap gets in the way when he's touching me. I can feel it around my throat. I am going to throw up. The strap broke. He made the strap break in my pocketbook and I am mad at him for that. He didn't care.* Snake was there, in the red pocketbook.

Jesus, I just want to throw up. It's that vertigo again. The up and down motion. And the strap is choking my neck and throat. And he broke the strap. I don't like the feeling of straps around my neck, my chest. It's my white undershirt too. The straps get pulled and twisted and dig into me. There are straps everywhere and they hurt.

What about the hands? The hands around my neck. That's as bad as the straps. Hands that go from my hips to my shoulders to my neck. Hands that hold my body in the right place while he goes up and down.

As sure as I am alive today, I am making this up. I know it. But I wish the nauseated head would go away. The tense muscles would go away. The tense cough would go away.

His hands are around my neck, on my collarbone. He has to push me back and forth to make it work. My face is so sore being open. My face is nauseated. I am coughing to get rid of it and tensing my chest and neck muscles to relieve the pain of his grip. Up and down and up and down. I feel sick. I can't hold on. I can't hold on.

Yes, I can. I can hold on to you. Now you are holding my hips. Up and down. Your grip is hurting me. It's all darkness, and I can't see anything. And I want to throw up. And I hold on to you. I can smell the cigarettes in your shirt pocket. My face rubs against them. They make me sick. Open my eyes. Camel cigarettes in your khaki shirt pocket. I am hot and sick and wet. You take care of me. You love me.

I have crawled into the hole. It's almost over and I can't see. I feel sick. I smell the cigarettes. I'm so sick. I want to disappear again. Please let me go away.

It was all too much. Where were these stories coming from? They couldn't be true. The distance between them and me felt like an unbridgeable chasm. Why would I want to bridge that chasm anyway? I closed my journal, turned off the light, and fell fast asleep.

The next Saturday morning, I drove forty-five minutes north of the city to a trail in the Pocono Mountains, intent on my purpose, dragging a backpack of thrift-shop chinaware behind me. Standing under a canopy of trees and next to a rolling brook, I stopped. The rage moved rapidly from my gut through my lungs and down my arms and legs, red hot like the summer sun hiding behind the collage of green, tan, black, brown, oval, round, irregular-shaped leaves. The unholy marriage of my dark past and irreconcilable present pulsed through the veins in my neck, my cheeks, my ears, so virile that my hair felt like it stood on end. The sounds of the moving water in front of my feet muffled the inner scream of knowing and unknowing, love and hate, terror and courage, sanity and, of course, insanity. I felt a knife silently slash my heart into a thousand pieces that reflected back the faces of my children, both real and inner parts of me. All that I loved was lost. I knew who to hate, even if I didn't. I knew who to blame, even if I didn't. This was my life and I only had one shot at it. If I didn't start over now, I never would. Maybe it was time to stop hating and blaming myself.

The red-and-yellow backpack was sitting on the ground. I leaned over, unzipped the bag, and retrieved one plate. I threw it against the rocks in the stream with all the force I could muster, watching the ceramics shatter into pieces and collapse into the running water. After a few more tries, one plate at a time wasn't enough, so I took two, then three and four plates at a time, listening to the crackle of the shards that fragmented into so many pieces, just like me. I screamed because nobody could hear me, and I screamed because I wanted everybody to hear me.

"I hate you. I hate you. I hate you," I yelled at the top of my lungs. I was returning the anger that was so often turned on me from the moment of my birth to this very slice of time. I changed course and stomped around the clearing, bringing each foot to earth with a force equal to the force of my rage. Tired from the energy I was expending and afraid I might break my toe, I began to throw the remaining dishes at a large tree whose stationary oneness stopped the abuse simply by being. I was dripping wet with beads of sweat and exhausted by the effort to measure out justice. I fell to the forest floor and dipped my hand in the water, taking breaths to bring me back to the present.

Mike knew how to manage rage. After he expelled it like a sonic explosion in outer space, he would take me home, have me deposit the shards of china into a trash bin, and let me rest. Then, he would push me toward socially acceptable action fueled by his fury. He was a genius.

CHAPTER 13

THE BATTLEFIELD

A dministration had its perks. I became principal of an elementary school with 550 students in a school district in the Lehigh Valley, situated several blocks from the college where John had just been offered a teaching position. My change in circumstance seemed to alter his whole perspective toward me. It probably didn't hurt that the children of some of his colleagues were students in the school I was administering. Whether it was due to his growth or my elevated status is up for question, but his vitriol subsided, and I took a sigh of relief. A year or so later, he married his second wife, Ann, and that clinched it. We were finally a couple of divorced parents who could stand to be in the same room together.

In truth, achieving this milestone took years on my part. Here again, John worked on his timetable, and I worked on mine, which was noticeably slower. He genuinely seemed to respect me and want to have a congenial, if distant, relationship, but it was hard to forget the dysfunctional dynamics between him, my parents, and me that were still active in the moment. I did my best to ignore the elephant in the living room so I could reach my goal, which was to become normal. If normal meant you could divorce and still be civil, then I would opt in that direction. In fits and starts, I was able to relate to John without crawling into victim mode inside. I didn't trust him, but I diligently practiced being pleasant to both him and his wife, Ann.

"Chuck, let's buy a house!" I said to my youngest son soon after I was hired to be the public-school principal. I wasn't rich, but I could manage it. Chuck was a junior in high school. He had completed his sophomore year at the therapeutic school and was reintegrating into his high school as an art major. His relationship with his dad had deteriorated, and he had moved in with a friend whose grandparents became his surrogate grandparents. Lizzy was attending college on John's benefits. Kimmy was living with friends and re-grounding herself after her emotional crisis and hospitalization. I was fifty years old, and it seemed like a good time to make the move into homeownership. I hoped Chuck would join me. He jumped at the chance.

"Cool, Mom. Yes! I'd love to live with you in a house."

We went to the realtor together and looked at several different properties in the small town where our story began. Chuck made the final call, an older, red-brick twin right in the center of town, in walking distance of almost everything. Not only had we agreed on our new home, but we worked together to spruce it up. The back steps to the house were rickety, and Chuck designed a very unique set of replacements that included a deck. We hired someone to build it, and later he and Lizzy put in pavers. Kimmy even joined us for a while in a very small third bedroom before beginning college herself.

Just a few blocks from the yellow-brick home we had left so many years ago, it felt like a whole new start. I was reunited with my children, I started a brand-new job, I owned my own home, and I felt more financially secure than I ever had before. It was, in miniature, a family reunion.

Nestled and safe in this little town, I looked around and realized I needed more form to my faith. I loved my Quaker roots and would always treasure them. But I wanted to experience the structure of a church service, to hear scripture spoken by someone who had spent hours praying over the meaning, and to move in concert with a liturgy. I found the largest church in walking distance from my house. One Sunday morning, I stepped nervously inside to the most beautiful service I could imagine at the United Church of Christ. There, I found a pastor who wove sermons with an artist's pallet and created visions of a world that was meant to be. Pastor Dan was exactly the pastoral presence I needed. He seemed safe and accessible, even fallible and imperfect. I began to attend regularly. Slowly, I became involved with extra-church activities like attending a healing prayer class and building homes in Honduras. I even led a women's retreat and discovered I was good at it. Church felt better and better.

One day, as a small church group was driving home from an event, Dan laughed and told me, "You're a little crazy like the rest of us. You'll fit in just fine."

What a relief to know it was okay to be less than perfect, to be crazy even. I'm sure Dan never knew how meaningful his joke was to this woman whose seemingly normal presentation belied her craziness. Perhaps his spiritual intuition prompted him to tell me that God loved me just the way I was—a message I surely needed to hear.

During Holy Week, the sanctuary was decorated with purple paraments, dark fabrics, and a cross draped in black. I was riveted by the movement from suffering and death to resurrection, a movement that was all too familiar to me. Later, Dan told me, "It was such a blessing for me to watch you experience Holy Week for the first time. So many of our longtime parishioners take it for granted. You were caught up in the story, and I could see it was moving you deeply. That was a gift to me and also to your neighbors in the pews. As you were moved, we were moved also. Thank you for reliving it for us."

At the time, I was traveling from my new home in the small town to see Sonia twice a week in the city, and journaling like mad. My position of authority as a school principal made me vulnerable to all manner of triggers that created plenty of raw material to bring into the therapy room. Bodily memories, pain, and exhaustion continued to ravage me, and Chuck and I had some anger issues to work out with each other.

Still, I began to see the tiniest possibility of a light at the end of the tunnel. I had a good job. I was reunited with my children. I had a church family. I had crossed the Rubicon from crazy to sane. Maybe, just maybe, I would one day be normal.

⌒

I don't like her, I blurted out in my journal. I was talking about Sara, a child sexual abuse survivor with DID who attended the weekly group Sonia facilitated.

I didn't like her the first day I saw her. I don't like her looks. She pushes her way in. She blurts out what she wants to say, and she doesn't think about the rest of us. It is like we don't exist, and we've lived through enough of not existing. She's very pushy. I shared my feelings with Sonia in an individual session. She told me that maybe the reason I didn't like Sara was because she reminded me of me. Really! I went home and ranted in my journal again.

Listen. I'm not pushy. I stay quiet in the background until there's danger. Then I get pushy. I don't know how she can hurt us, but I think she can. It's like she doesn't even listen to what she's saying herself. First, she's pissed because she wants to see everybody's abreactions—then she flips out when someone has a five-minute flashback. She switches all the time and I'm afraid of her alters. I was furious that Sonia had the nerve to compare me with Sara. *You think I'm like her, but I'm not like her. I'm angry like her, but she's out of control.*

Over time I began to understand what Sonia was telling me. When we see our dark side in another, we are repulsed—we hate the other person so we don't have to hate ourselves. This is one manifestation of what psychologists call transference.

I attended group for an hour and a half once a week for six years. During that time, almost every woman there became an object of *transference* for me, the term used to describe the act of a person redirecting some of their feelings about one person onto an entirely different person. For a while, Sara was my father; then she was my sister, then my mother, then my father again. Other members, too, triggered my transference response. This made group an extremely painful experience—not the warm, fuzzy support I had found in the women's unit.

In some weird way, I reenacted my abuse in group. Of course, no one was abusing me, but you couldn't convince my alters of that. To protect myself from the trauma I imagined was happening in group, I believed I had to convey strength for my own survival. *Weakness—I can't show weakness,* I wrote in my journal with passive influence from the Devil. *Weakness is bad. I can't let the group see my weakness. If I make a mistake or say something untrue or make a faulty analysis or assumption, I can't let them know—or they will think I am weak. Weakness is death. I must be strong. Better to be angry than to show any weakness,* I continued. *You can imagine how hard it is just to write this. It's admitting weakness, that I might be wrong, not right, that I might be dirty. But right this very moment, I don't feel dirty. Maybe that's because I wrote it. But I still feel intense pain. My whole body aches. I can hardly move.*

In some of the few moments I was able to share honestly what was going on with group members, they wondered why I continued to attend. I wondered too. I didn't stop. I went into the lion's den each week.

The old brick schoolhouse was massive, situated in the west end of the city where the educated people lived, surrounded by a playing field protected by a chain-link fence and the residential homes of the middle class. It was a monument to a day gone by when education, students, and teachers fit in a neat box. Historically, the school had lived up to the privilege of teaching the sons and daughters of college professors, doctors, lawyers and such, and its reputation was stellar, even as the demographics changed. Now about a third of the school had shifted, and the children of drug addiction, domestic violence, and poverty would settle their differences with their wealthier playmates on the playground. The school was undergoing massive changes, but I didn't know that yet.

"Becky, have a seat," I said, pointing to a makeshift chair in my office, edged in between boxes of envelopes and parent letters informing families what classroom their students were assigned to in September. It was midsummer, my second week at the school as principal, and most of the teachers were away.

"Thank you for coming in." The mailings belonged in the main office but had found their way into mine because the new secretarial staff person hired before I had arrived didn't know how to alphabetize, and the wrong letters had been inserted into the wrong envelopes. All 550 of them.

"You're the first person to take me up on my offer to visit and share our hopes and dreams," I told Becky. I had sent each teacher a letter and invited them to visit for a chat and a cup of tea when they had time. "Tell me about yourself, about the school, your joys, and your concerns."

Becky, the consummate professional, sat amid the mess and told me she was a fifth-grade teacher. She was nice enough to give me some history of the school, the building, and the "must know" teachers who were the experts on certain things. "What are you most proud of?" I asked.

"The fifth-grade team has been together a long time. We work so well. I don't think there's a child we can't reach if we all pitch in to problem-solve," she said.

"Wonderful. I'm so glad to hear that. Do you have any concerns?"

Becky wiggled in her chair. She looked at her hands, the floor, the walls. Her silence was deadening. The air was so thick I could slice it.

Finally, she looked at me and said, "Oh, no. Nothing." We exchanged a few more pleasantries and then Becky got up to go. On her way out the door, she glanced back. "You might want to check out school-wide discipline." Then she disappeared.

As it turned out, the school was rife with conflict born of a site-based faction that had grown out of the previous school-level administration. The once-cohesive staff was split apart by parents and some administrators who had allied together to push the school in a particular teaching direction. Favoritism had been rampant, and teachers had been pitted against each other. No one on the district-level team who hired me had said a word about conflict. I walked with my eyes closed right into the middle of a battlefield. I greeted the conflict with resolve, but underneath the surface, my alters were shaking in their shoes. How was I going to handle this?

⌒

Group was another battlefield in my life. I declared to Sonia I would never go back to group, or I would confront the people who posed danger in the room. Sometimes, I crawled into a ball in my bed for hours on end before group met. Usually, my body pulsed with pain in anticipation. After group was over, I called the suicide prevention hotline on more than one occasion. Week after week, month after month, year after year, I struggled with my fear of each member and of the whole group, together, as a unit. They had the power to hurt me, or so I thought. Analyzing every person in group, I wrote my assessment of them in my journal.

A, it feels to me like you are drawn to Sara the way you are drawn to your abusive husband. Sara is familiar to you and somehow you think she will protect you. I was terrified I would be drawn into taking care of A in the same way I had taken care of my mother, who was drawn in by my father.

B, you make me angry because I expected so much more from you. Where are your real feelings? You said you make nice and it pisses me off. B was strong like my sister, but I didn't know who she really was. Was she safe or would she hurt me in the end?

C, it's hard to explain how I feel about you. Uncomfortable is the best word I can find. I don't want your help. You can't fix me. I only want your respect. C was so nice to everyone I was afraid she would deny the abuse the way everyone in my family denied the abuse, and I would get hurt.

D, AKA Sara. I hate you. You have this group running. Nobody wants to make anybody upset, everyone wants friends, so this group is open game for you. I was furious she controlled the group the way my father controlled our family.

Danger lurked everywhere, so I created multiple battle plans.

Plan A: For me to continue in group, I will have to tell each person exactly how I feel about them. I cannot, will not, continue to function in a dysfunctional unit that emulates my family. I will ask Rosie to try to stay at home. Survivor will have to do the talking, which means I will be shut off from feelings. But Mike has to stay right by her side in case feelings creep in. This will be a week-by-week decision, a week-by-week effort. It may not work. Believe me, if I walk out of group the way Sara did, I will not come back. And I think I'm going to stop socializing. No more after-group snacks. Why pretend? It just pulls me down into the dysfunction more, brings out my alters who are needy, makes me vulnerable, and enmeshes me. This is a tough road, but I am the one who is walking it, and I want to get better. So maybe I will just have to go it alone. Fuck friendship.

Plan B: Scrap the confrontation. Confrontation, even moderate discussion, puts too many of us (alters) *at risk. What if we can't pull it off? I have to negotiate inside what my function and role will be in this group, and what function and role the group will play in my life. Rosie, Sylvia, and others want friends: this group will not provide you with friends at this point. For us, the purpose of group is to learn how to create conditions for safe relationships. Right now, we are paving the way. Setting boundaries. This is for our own good. Paula–Survivor can point out dysfunctions as they come up. Maintain distance. Survivor, you and Paula can act like you're involved but stay out of it. Stay strong to keep emotions out. In time, group dysfunction may decrease, and others may be allowed to attend. So then, it's settled. Paula–Survivor will attend group. No children are allowed. Sylvia, you can slide in there if you feel safe enough, but only in conjunction with Paula. She's in control.*

With the focus of a highly trained combat team, I watched for every possible line of attack, every surprise ambush, any IED that might blow up at the slightest wrong move. I was terrified. Unlike real combat teams, I totally lacked confidence in my ability to navigate the land mines.

Once I informed the district-level administration of the volatile situation at the school, they put lots of resources into resolving the conflict. Sure, they had known something was going on, but they decided not to delve further until I came on the scene. One of the departments spent months working with focus groups to enable parents and teachers to share their feelings honestly about what was going on.

"Lyn, the best way we can help this school community heal is to give everyone a chance to be heard. This will protect you from the fallout of the previous administration and help you move the school forward," said the department director. This was music to my ears. The director shared my view of grieving and healing. I knew we could work together well.

"I can't tell you how happy I am that you feel that way. I don't think there's any way I could work through this complicated conflict with the whole community by myself. Tell me what to do and I'll do it."

"We wouldn't hang you out to dry, Lyn," he said, chuckling under his breath. "We want you to succeed. Here's how we'll go about it." The department director proceeded to lay out his thorough and insightful plan. The report they produced was important but not nearly as important as the process of speaking and listening.

For my part, I remained open to listening to parent and teacher concerns while I established equitable sharing of power, curriculum development, and a school-wide discipline plan. I discovered later that the district had hired me because they believed my experience with Quaker consensus would help me manage a site-based school, especially one with conflict.

For whatever reason, conflict seemed to follow me around. Although I had not been successful at resolving conflicts with my ex-husband or my parents, I had learned a lot from those still ongoing experiences. I was in the middle of grave conflict in group therapy and hadn't figured a way through that morass. Conflict with my children was raw but healing, and I believed that was because I did everything in my power to understand where they were coming from and meet them wherever they were. Inner conflict with and between my alters was settling down as I learned more and more how to love them. To the best of my ability, I brought those multilevel layers of conflict experience in my personal life to help heal school conflict. At my core, I believed conflict explored and resolved would result in deeper, healthier relationships.

"Conflict that deepens, not conflict that divides," I said at faculty meetings. "It's normal, even healthy to have different opinions. Let's make sure those differences don't cause us to split as a faculty. Let's expect we can learn from each other, no matter how different we are."

There were many triggers for me to maneuver, but the most illuminating moment was more of an epiphany than a trigger. People in power could be real. They could be difficult and deceitful, but they could also be kind and compassionate.

It is very scary to think of people, I wrote in my journal. *They are so scary. It is especially scary to see them breathe, smile, be nice and kind, then be powerful, then be not perfect. So amazing. So amazing. Especially with powerful people. They have skin. They have feelings. They breathe. They puzzle over things. They overeat. They get ticked off. They make mistakes. They are just like me.*

Ironically, everyone saw me as powerful, but I still saw myself as powerless.

"Yap, yap, yap, yap, yap, yap, yap, yap, yap," was all I could hear. The sound reverberated behind my ears like a big drum calling me to war. Sara was looking straight at me in the middle of group therapy and blaming me for something I didn't do. *How dare she?* I thought. *Here we go again,* and I looked for the words that would stop her in her tracks. No such luck. "Yap, yap, yap," it continued. The rest of the group watched the two of us battling it out again.

In the bowels of my brain, Snake said, *You don't have to take this. I'm tired of hearing her scream. Pour your soda on her head. That will shut her up.* Mike got up, walked over to Sara, and did Snake's bidding.

This created a big to-do, of course. Sara—hair wet with Diet Coke—jumped up and hit me on the arm. Everyone sat there shocked with their mouths open, and Sonia stepped between the two of us to make sure I didn't hit back. *Really? Did I just pour my soda on Sara?* I wondered with surprise and a little bit of awe. Sara's punch was hard enough to produce a bruise, which I discovered the next day when I was bathing. Two days later, I had a previously scheduled doctor's appointment, and he noticed the bruise too. Needless to say, this incident ended group for that night.

We all had a lot of inner work and soul-searching to do to process what had happened. Sonia set new rules in place for group participation. I went into catatonic pain interspersed with arguing with Sonia, who I was sure had not protected me, and journaling about my role in this terrible situation.

Honestly, I could barely remember any of it. Sonia told me we were sitting in group having a reasonable discussion about whether out-of-group incidents between members of the group could be brought into the group setting to resolve. In my opinion, Sara was spouting her theories about what was right and what was wrong, and, in her opinion, I was wrong. At least, that's how I heard it. I conflated Sara's premise that I was "wrong" with my own belief that I was "bad." It put me on high alert. To me, Sara seemed unfair, over-the-top angry, and dangerous. As I processed what happened, Sonia held my feet to the fire so I would own my part. There was no doubt I had escalated the affair. At least Sonia affirmed my memory that Sara was screaming at me. *She's screaming at me!*

In the end, Paula used her brilliant logic to figure things out. In many ways, it was a turning point for me in understanding and managing my relationships in group and in the rest of the world. This was Paula's assessment:

> *This is what I know. I know I was afraid of Sara and put some*
> *of the Devil's shame on her because it was too much for him to bear*

alone. So when I was terrified of group I was really terrified of my own shame. I felt it in the fear, but I would not acknowledge it in my mind. It had to be hers for me to survive in that moment.

Now I am beginning to acknowledge my own shame in my mind. I am beginning to accept it as my own. I have not fully accepted it, but I am beginning to. I wonder if I <u>had</u> to pour soda on Sara so I could begin to accept it? I can't escape responsibility for that.

It has been very painful. The pain has been excruciating. It is deadly to face your own shame. It is so incapacitating (I want to commit suicide!) that I have to start to let go of it for the time being. It will come back again, I'm sure.

Here is something else I know. When I put my shame on Sara (or anyone else), I am doing what John has done with me. I am giving it away because I can't bear to carry it all myself. John accuses me of all that he is because he can't carry his shame himself.

Because I, Paula, am beginning to acknowledge and accept the shame does not mean the others are. But this is a first step. I am the mind. This is all mind work that grows from the soil of the inner work. But the inner work is ongoing. The Devil is still hiding. Rosie is crying. Little Lynn wants to dig in her heels. Mike is ready to build a wall between us and the rest of the world. And Snake is still laughing. But the Protector has covered them with a blanket of quiet, peace, and love, and told them to rest for now. It has been very hard on them. And now I can hold down the fort while they rest.

Snake is not going to do it again. But he's glad he got to do it just once.

~

By transferring onto group members, then taking my responses back to Sonia to process, I began to heal my dysfunction in relationships. I learned through agonizing interactions that I didn't need to hate someone or fear them. Slowly and with trepidation, I gained confidence in my ability to navigate different people and different personalities, and I learned that I wasn't as vulnerable as I thought I was. What started out as an explosive microcosm of my family under a microscope ended up as an opportunity to explore honest intimacy. I hated group, and then I loved it, or at least I learned to love many of the other women who attended. Without group, I would never have learned how to have strong, healthy relationships. It took years, however, and slow, agonizing inner exploration.

Toward the end of my healing journey, I attended an arts retreat where we used metal, wood, and metal-working tools to create something of meaning. My artwork embodied two brief poems I had written, one about my pain and one about group:

> *Red burst forth in anger and pain*
> *While black creeps out to fill the cracks*
> *Then covers all*
> *Dead center*
> *Dead.*

And:

> *They were in the cradle with me.*
> *They rocked the cradle.*
> *They held the mirror up as I screamed in agony to see myself.*
> *Then they rocked the cradle.*

Drawing from my earlier poem, I brought my angst into group where they rocked me in a metaphorical cradle. The people in group rocked me not because they liked me but because it was their role. We rocked each other in odd and often reluctant ways. Still, their presence required me to see my shadow, which both devastated and healed me. With this piece of art, I gave thanks to group in ambivalence and appreciation.

PART 3

Glow Upon The Beach

1998 AND BEYOND

Glow Upon the Beach

There are pebbles at the beach that are as smooth as ice.
They tell me that the polished, glassy surface of these rocks was pounded
out of their own ragged edges by the tumultuous weight of the raging ocean
over eons of time.

Rolling along the depths of the ocean floor,
caught up in the spiraling currents,
tossed about in an underwater web of chaos,
now and then riding the crest of the wave,
then smashing against the saturated earth

not once, not twice
but so many times,
so many cycles of abuse,
of pain and horror,
reliving,
healing,
breathing once again
to produce this rosy gem, this pebble over time,
that cups within my hand.

My hand protects the tiny stone,
appreciates the wisdom trapped within this body,
delights in the touch, the shape, the feel of the nugget
but can never take away the history
or the polish
which is only the result
of the pounding
and the pain
and the pounding

and the pain
and the pounding
and the pain.

And so to you, God, I offer this pebble over time
whose glow upon the beach
reveals not
the journey from whence it came.

July 2004

CHAPTER 14

WHEN 10 + 10 = ONE

When I began to attend the United Church of Christ, my spirituality deepened further. One spring day, at the age of fifty-one, I drove the rural back roads through Bucks County into Montgomery County to attend a Saturday-morning workshop at our conference center. It focused on the theme of gratitude. I honestly wasn't sure what gratitude was, but I was willing to learn.

"As we begin today," said Wanda, the minister of spiritual nurture, "let's focus ourselves on prayer and remember what we feel grateful for in this very moment." About fifteen of us sat on chairs arranged in a circle in the large gathering room. We closed our eyes and relaxed our bodies as she led us through a guided meditation meant to illuminate our inner places of thanksgiving. I closed my eyes, then opened them to see if I was doing this right. I looked at a painting of the risen Christ, then down at my hands, then around the room at everyone else, who seemed deeply engrossed in prayer. I had no idea what I was grateful for and no comprehension of what I was supposed to do. With all that was on my plate, I seemed to have no space for this mysterious state of being called gratitude.

As the meditation came to an end, everyone opened their eyes with a smile and sense of peace, presumably with some clarity about God's goodness in their lives. One by one, we went around the room and shared.

"The sunrise outside my kitchen window."

"My daughter, who's visiting us this weekend."

"My mother is better after a difficult illness."

My mind panicked as I heard the responses come closer and closer to me. What would I say? How would I manage this? Why didn't I feel grateful when everyone else did? Proof, once again, that I was crazy, defective, not normal.

"Honestly, Wanda, I don't know what to say," I offered in shame when it was my turn. "I'm in a difficult place right now. I'm finding it hard to be grateful for anything." I waited for stunned silence, shunning, disbelief.

Instead, Wanda didn't miss a beat.

"Lyn, thank you so much for your honesty! It's true for all of us that sometimes we just can't get in touch with gratitude for all the burdens we are carrying. God knows your challenges and is here to help you. You have helped us by your honesty, giving us permission to be honest about our real feelings too."

Just like that, I was affirmed. Just like that, I was un-shamed. Just like that, I was welcomed into this group of normal people who weren't shocked by my lack of gratitude. I left the class realizing that I *was* grateful. I had been given a gift that drew forth my gratitude—the gift of acceptance.

Becoming normal continued to be a goal, but over the years I learned that there is no such animal, and that while everyone was not abused as a child, everyone does have burdens to carry. Everyone does have negative, unhappy feelings. Everyone does get to the end of their rope now and again. After my years of deep healing and my plunge into spiritual growth, I even learned that sometimes I had more resilience and wisdom than normal people with less challenging pasts. The "courage, strength, and wisdom to know myself and do your will" prayer that sustained me through my chaos was paying off.

For many years, I wrote, *Help me, help me, help me,* over and over in my journal, not knowing who I was writing to or even why I was asking for help. As time went on, I noticed a slow but monumental shift. I began writing, *Thank you, thank you, thank you.*

This time, I knew I was writing to God.

At the school, the conflict faded into the background, and teachers learned to respect each other, just as I had hoped. Truthfully, it was an honor to work with them. They were energetic, filled with enthusiasm, and set high standards, even for their students who demonstrated the most difficult behaviors. One of the teachers became a push-in support who helped students, teachers, and parents navigate the challenging issues. She supported everyone as we managed the changing cultural dynamics.

"You turn yourselves into pretzels to make these kids learn," I told them at a faculty meeting. "I'm so proud of you and proud of this school. If a child can't make it here, they can't make it anywhere."

Serving as principal was a grounding mechanism for me. Even though the job itself triggered me, going back out into the school community reminded me I really was competent and capable. It brought me into the present when my insiders were hurting from the past. Still, the level of energy required from me to do the job right left me with few resources for myself or my insiders. I knew I was doing a good job, but I wondered how long I could maintain it.

I looked at "my" school with joy. Primary teachers were using state-of-the-art language-arts strategies to teach their children to read. Intermediate teachers were writing curriculum that expected the best from their students. The primary and intermediate wings were cross-fertilizing. A gifted art teacher integrated multicultural arts across curriculum in all grade levels, and the school became a demonstration site for the county. It was a vibrant school community with engaged teachers, students, and parents. I was a part of it. I was grateful.

Face it head on, Mike had instructed me in my journal. *Face it head on. Face it head on. Face it head on. Face it head on. Face it head on.* He was giving me written instructions about how to cope with my complicated and painful life. The old educational maxim held true: repetition is the mother of learning. Since Mike shared my body with a teacher, he knew he had to repeat his commandment over and over again if it was going to stick.

With Sonia's help, I had explored debilitating triggers, dove straight into excruciating relationship dysfunction, and tackled career advancement in the midst of emotional turmoil. I had learned to love my alters and allowed them ample airtime to express their fear, rage, and grievances in spite of the fact their stories seemed disconnected to my perception of reality. I had worked hard to nurture bonds with my real children that had been damaged by my descent downwards, my inner chaos, and the debilitating symptoms of dissociation.

Yet in spite of eight years of hard work, I still had no explicit memories, memories that would document actual events. Most of the stories I was given by my alters remained distant, pseudo-fictitious, as if they were happening to someone else. My perpetrator was always "he," not a name or even a clear image. I felt his invasion but hid his personhood. Yes, I had unreal fragments I found hard to believe. Yes, I had stories of terror, shame, and rage. But no, I had nothing I could define as clear, cognitive memories.

Although Mike was the force that kept moving me forward in recovery, he was not a fan of unearthing traumatic memories and turning them into indisputable facts. He was quite satisfied to let my knowledge of past events remain implicit—that is, controlled by the back brain and stored in my body where they remained physical sensations, fragments, snippets, and emotional responses. Joining Mike in this campaign to withhold specific details of trauma were Protector and No Name, who had told me they would never tell. They insisted my system had been set up in such a way as to hide the knowledge forever. I wanted to know exactly what happened, but my alters had banded together to keep me in the dark.

"You have traumatic memories, Lyn," explained Sonia. "Trauma isn't just a frightening experience; it's the perception of mortal danger. When you were little, you perceived your life was threatened, and your brain responded the way any brain would—by activating your fight, flight, or freeze response. Your body never lies," she went on. "That's why your body hurts, and you only have little snippets instead of full-on memory. Your brain chose a creative coping strategy by splitting off the memories into separate parts so you could go on living in spite of the horror you experienced. The stories your alters have told you seem distant and unreal because they are stored in the back brain, the emotional brain, that kicks in when trauma occurs. The traumatic events you experienced never made it to the front brain, the thinking brain, the part of your brain where explicit memories live."

I still wasn't satisfied, so I argued with my alters and explained the value of learning what happened to make me multiple. I believed, if they cooperated, my implicit memories would make the journey to my front brain where they would become real to me. I wanted my memories to move from my body to my thinking brain so I would have an explanation of why I went crazy for a significant period of my life. I didn't want fuzzy fragments and generalized body pain. I wanted memories that would prove I wasn't crazy without a shadow of a doubt.

Late one night, I sat in my bed with my journal in hand, my stuffed animals Mike, Rosie, and Devil in comfortable positions around my comforter. My preparations for school were done and in my tote bag, so I had time to present my case to whomever in my system didn't want me to remember. I puffed up my pillows, sank into their softness, and began to write.

Little Lynn surprised me by taking the lead. She was certain memory retrieval was not in our best interest. *We've managed all these years, haven't we? We were good, we followed the rules. Now this body is getting so naughty. Some of you have already leaked too much. We're going to get in trouble; you know that, don't you? You are all being so bad and doing bad things. Telling what happened is a bad thing. Why can't you be good? I'm good. I do what I'm supposed to do. And I don't know anything. And I don't want to know anything. I don't want to get into trouble. I don't know what will happen to me if I do, but I don't want to find out. That's why I've always been so good, you know.*

I had a ready argument to convince her that things were different now, that I was a grown-up, that we wouldn't get hurt, that we deserved to know the truth. *Don't you see we won't get into trouble? We're grown up now, and we're allowed to do what's right for us and know the truth. The truth won't hurt us. It will heal us.*

Little Lynn was not convinced. *Pain hurts and I don't want to hurt. I don't want pain. Nanny has pain and Rosie has pain. That's why Rosie and I separated, so I wouldn't have to feel the pain. I don't want to hurt.*

I tried to be empathetic and look at it from her point of view. *I don't know, I guess it will hurt a lot to know. But if we spread it out, maybe it won't hurt so much. And then, they say, the hurt will get better and we'll get better.*

Of course, Mike had to weigh in too. *You're fucking crazy to think this isn't going to hurt. These kids, all of us, have been through a lot. You want us to go through it again? You're crazy. The experts don't know what you would need to know to experience it. They may be right in theory, but they don't know us. Amnesia has its strong points, and I, for one, am not in favor of giving it up.*

I was tired and had nothing else up my sleeve. *I can't think of any more good arguments now, but we'll need to talk about this some more. Please think about it. And maybe we can talk to Sonia about it.*

Mike turned out the light and said, *"Fuck Sonia."*

After eight years of sitting in a circle for an hour and a half a week, pouring out our guts, sometimes challenging each other and sometimes supporting each other, our therapy group disbanded. Some of the participants had moved on in their healing, and others dropped out for other reasons. I had mixed feelings. What would we do without each other? Who would I transfer onto? Did I even need to transfer onto anyone anymore? I had worked through my issues with group and had less fear and more appreciation of other group members. I would have liked to continue friendships. A few of us were left to commiserate at Friendly's after a session.

"We don't even like each other, so why am I feeling sad?" I asked, dipping into my hot fudge sundae with a smile.

"Because underneath we do like each other," said Joan as she sipped on her ice cream soda, egging me on. "We've walked the same journey. You can't get as far as we have together without caring." She grinned at me, blowing to pieces my brutal experience of the lion's den.

"Yeah, we'll never forget each other," said Alicia. She nibbled around her single scoop. Always the peacemaker, she was building a bridge we would hang on to when our formal work together was over. "We're still here for each other. Let's remember that."

Members of group had come and gone. Sara and I had negotiated an invisible truce, and though we never became close friends, we could respect each other for who we were. Joan, Alicia, and I had been there almost from the beginning, and each of us had come to a turning point in our lives. In spite of my complaints, we were ready to move on.

I continued to work with Sonia individually, but my sessions were less dissociative and more about managing my career and planning for the future. That raw feeling—the tuning fork that assured me I had touched on some important truth—happened less frequently. Conflicting voices in my head were giving way to one mind thinking things through from different perspectives. I was rarely numb and began to feel the full range of emotions anyone might feel. The shimmering icicles retired as I felt real and present almost all the time.

Occasional triggers popped up, but I was learning how to manage by myself with just a little bit of coaching from Sonia. I knew, for instance, that a trigger would last almost twenty-four hours, on the nose, from start to finish. I knew the incidents that caused me to trigger were legitimately concerning, but my responses were over the top. I knew my most effective grounding technique was getting back out there and interacting with people where I would feel competent and capable again. Life was not perfect, but my ability to function, trust myself, and live with less pain, fear, and shame grew by leaps and bounds. I was trending toward normal.

I'm acting and feeling like a normal person, I thought as I walked out of Sonia's office after a therapy session. *Maybe this is what therapy feels like for the rest of the world. Maybe I won't need therapy much longer.*

"I'm impatient, Sonia," I said at our next session. "I want to live. I want to love. I want to grow. I don't want to sit around and wait for memories that may never come."

"Lyn, I think that's exactly what all your work has been about. Learning how to live. And you're doing a magnificent job!"

I drove up a wooded hill in the northern part of the county to Thelma's beautiful home. It had been almost ten years since she dropped me off at the women's unit at Northwestern Institute. Her property was lush, covered with laurels, rhododendrons, oaks, maples, and pine. I parked my car under the trees and made my way across the cobbled driveway, thinking how long it had been since I had seen my friend who stood by me in the most vulnerable time of my life.

"Lyn, it's so good to see you," Thelma exclaimed as she threw open her door, wrapping me in a big hug. With her usual hospitable demeanor, she welcomed me into her home so we could catch up.

"I want to hear about everything," Thelma said. She prepared a pot of tea for the two of us. Widowed since before I had met her, she had just retired and was beginning a term as board member in a local school district. Thelma's healing journey had been different from mine. She spent considerable time processing her traumatic memories, and unlike me, she remembered her trauma clearly. I settled in on her screened-in porch as we shared with each other the highlights of our lives.

"When I think about it, Thelma, I realize the breakup of my marriage was the trigger that tore my alters apart. Until that time, my parts worked well together most of my life—so well that I never knew they were there until the shock of my divorce ripped me apart. Then everyone split off, and I decompensated."

We finished our tea and got up to take a walk around the property. "How are your kids?" Thelma asked "Did you ever figure out what was going on with your children? I remember how worried you were about them but how impotent you felt when you tried to help. You always seemed to blame yourself."

"They're doing okay, Thelma. They have the same ups and downs all young adults have, but, for the most part, they're figuring their lives out. You know, it turned out that the part of me who was such a good mother was an alter," I explained. "Her name is Laura. She was starting to get shaky even before I learned of John's affair because I think she felt, intuitively, that all was not right in paradise. My student-teaching experience was a warning sign that had nothing to do with my marriage. But the affair and all the difficulties working with John reminded her too much of the original betrayal. She just disappeared. Vamoose! My kids were left with a mother who lost her mothering chops." I picked up a branch from the ground and threw it into the woods. "I learned, again, how to mother, but my children lost a lot of me. It had to have affected them badly. I think John's own decompensation and our terrible conflict didn't help either."

"None of us are perfect, Lyn. Don't get me going on my own family! You did the best you could with what you had. And your kids are resilient. They'll have their own healing journeys to take as their lives move on. So, tell me, did Laura ever return?" We stopped for a few moments in the shade of a tall maple and breathed in the scent of honeysuckle. Breathing, when you've lived a dissociative life for many years, can sometimes feel like an act of God.

"Well, sure. She was always around a little bit with the children I taught, but even there she sometimes slipped away. Laura is so loving but very sensitive. I think her love is authentic and deep, but the love she experienced as a child was hurtful. 'They' loved her, then they hurt her, so she was very confused. At the least whiff of danger, she was out of there." I stopped for a few moments to reflect on the consequences. "She's learning how to love her adult children, which is a whole different ball of wax from loving little toddlers! And now that I'm a grandmother, she's testing her wings with my grandson too."

Tears welled in my eyes as we shared the tales of our unlikely journeys. I grieved, in that moment, all I had lost in the family I created. The deep bonds that molded me to my children, through Laura, had become a lifeline in my early adulthood and motherhood. They defined me when I otherwise had no definition. When my system broke apart, the bonds with my children broke apart too, damaging all of us. I could never regain that but spent the better part of my life trying to repair it. I had loved before and I would love again, but no love, ever, would come close to the raw, fiery love I had for my children.

The sun was high in the sky, and we both knew I would be leaving soon. It had been a wonderful afternoon of reminiscing and comparing notes. Our walk meandered around her expansive property, and we ended up in her driveway where my car waited. With our busy lives, we knew we might not talk again for another long stretch of time. More to the point, I was thinking about going to seminary, which would take me further from her than I already was. It seemed like we needed to bless each other as we celebrated our emergence from the long tunnel of dissociative pain into lives of coherence and peace.

"Thelma, I'm not crazy anymore."

"Good to know, Lyn. I'm not either!"

"It's kind of amazing to look back on my life to see how it evolved. How I evolved. Not only am I sane, I'm happy!"

"The hard work of confronting the past really pays off, doesn't it?" Thelma spoke with a sly smile that betrayed the secrets we both shared. "We've been through a lot, haven't we?"

"We sure have," I agreed. "But look at us. We're here! We're survivors!"

"No," she corrected me. "We're thrivers!"

The integration of my alters into my whole self was never in question. From the beginning, they seemed to be in agreement that we wanted to be one whole human being. *Someday, I will be integrated,* I wrote in my journal. *What a wonderful thought. What a wonderful feeling.*

Mike was nostalgic. *No, I will be sad to lose all these little ones. We are so much a part of each other. We are friends, family, we keep each other company. You too. We are your purpose, and you are our purpose. We will miss you when we integrate. You will be all alone. We all love you and each other so much.*

As I began to engage in relationships with other people in healthy ways, my insiders' need to express fear, anger, and other negative emotions diminished. They basked in good feelings when I had success in my personal life. Slowly and gradually, they spoke less and less. *When you all come together, when you find your places in the puzzle, you will not go away,* I insisted to Mike. *You will all be a part of me, a part of the whole me. I will cry with happiness when we are all together. You will not disappear,* I reassured myself and everyone else.

Over the summer after visiting Thelma, I took my vacation alone at a bed-and-breakfast on Martha's Vineyard. I drove up I-95 along the Eastern Seaboard, then caught the ferry from Woods Hole to Oak Bluffs. The sun was blistering hot, just the way I liked it. Day after day, I strolled along the beaches, browsed through the shops, and basked in the sun. Each afternoon, the sounds of the ocean rolled over my inner landscape as I sat in my beach chair and watched gulls and sandpipers compete for bits of food hidden in the sand. Waves that looked ominous from a distance petered out as they broke, their frothy foam lapping just inches from my toes. The sun baked my consciousness into meditative suspension. The sounds of the ocean beat in rhythm with my heart. Massaging me. Soothing me. Healing me.

There is a new me here at the ocean. Out of my suspended state, words flowed into the journal I had packed into my beach bag. *There is still a feeling of uncertainty, worry, and fear of the unknown but also a feeling of peace. I am mostly together. Did you know that, now, we are all together?* I asked myself. *My parts make up all of me, so it's a familiar feeling. But now they are a part of me together. They are "integrated." We are integrated. I am integrated. Some of us have grown up, and some of us have remained children, but my parts are all a part of the big puzzle that is me. It took a long time to put the pieces together, but they fit nicely,* I marveled. Without letting me know, my alters had completed what we all set out to do, on their own. *I'm one big puzzle that's all put together.*

I closed my journal, wiggled my toes in the sand, then stood and stretched in the shadow of the late-afternoon sun. I gathered my belongings and walked back to my bed-and-breakfast, dragging my beach chair behind me. The nice man who owned the lodging was happy to chat for a while as we shared small stories of our lives. I was getting hungry, so he directed me to a cozy little restaurant for a sumptuous seafood dinner. When night fell, I climbed into the big cushy bed and read a chapter of the book on my nightstand. I breathed deeply and gently. It was a good vacation. Quiet, renewing, peaceful. I closed my eyes and gave thanks that out of many, I became one.

And that's the way it's been for decades. Now and then, someone breaks away for a few moments to speak through my voice or tell me what they think. But mostly, they trust me. Rosie, Mike, Sylvia, Laura, Paula, Devil, Snake, Victim, Survivor, Black Knight, No Name, Protector, and the other parts who formed the whole of me. When I counted the *fragments* of personality I met over the years, along with my foundational parts, there were nigh on twenty. They will always be there because that's the way my brain was formed in those developmental, traumatic years of my life. They did their work, and now we were one.

EPILOGUE

In 2001, at the age of fifty-four, I would enroll in Lancaster Theological Seminary and spend three years immersed in theology, biblical studies, Christology, pastoral counseling, and more. I would serve two churches and become a certified spiritual director. In retirement, I volunteered for an organization called Gestalt Pastoral Care (www.gestaltpastoralcare.org), whose holistic approach to healing helped me tie up some loose therapeutic ends. The Iraq War, the election of the first African American as president of the United States, and a global pandemic were the backdrop to my busy life, but the wide expanse of a pain-free, drama-free existence was breathtakingly front and center. The seeds of gratitude planted at Wanda's retreat years ago had taken root, and I found myself in a veritable garden of grace.

To be clear, life was not perfect in those years post-integration, and I experienced a number of painful losses. Both my parents died. I didn't grieve their deaths at the time because I had already grieved that loss over ten-plus years of inner work. I married a wonderful man in 2008, and he died unexpectedly in 2009 just four days before our first anniversary. *The grief is great, but the gratitude is greater*, I wrote to a hundred family members and friends in an email I sent on the night of his death. I lost a church I loved through surprising and unexpected circumstances. Although most of my children made wonderful lives for themselves, one continued to struggle. I trudged along doing what God seemed to be calling me to do, what my inner healing compass was urging me to do, and what all of me and my integrated parts wanted to do.

Over the years, John and I came to a place of peace. Together, we forged a good, if distant, relationship, bound together by the beautiful children we produced and the grandchildren we adored. The gruesome end to our marriage may not have been all his fault, but I could finally say it wasn't all my fault either. We both made big mistakes, but we both did the best we could within the constraints of our limitations. And he chose well the second time around when he married Ann, who has loved our adult children as if they were her own.

"Happy Birthday, Lizzy!" we all sang happily at a family reunion in the Pocono Mountains to celebrate Lizzy's fortieth birthday. It was the first time in decades our whole family had gotten together, paving the way for birthday reunions to become a family tradition for all of our children. My car got stuck on the unpaved, ice-covered, mountainous road on the way to the retreat, but our family became unstuck as we sat around the big old fireplace and reignited family ties.

Ron and I met when I was sixty-seven years old. He became my faithful, loving husband and my solid-as-a-rock friend. We settled in Upstate New York between the Adirondack Mountains and Lake Champlain, near one of my children with a spouse and grandchildren. How cool was that?! Laura, safe at last, was thrilled. Across the country, five grandchildren and one great-grandchild decorated my heart. Not only did I achieve my goal of becoming normal, I succeeded at my shot at happiness as well.

Many, many years ago, shortly after I had separated from John, the beautiful mother of one of my students asked me, "Lyn, are you happy?" We had bumped into each other on our separate walks in the downtown of our local community. I couldn't help but notice that her eyes were piercing, like bright-blue gems reflecting the depths of an azure sea, yet they were calm, confident, clear. Her own husband had just started serving prison time for selling marijuana. That was enough to create a storm in anyone's life. For all I knew, they had been a normal, middle-class family, but here she was, alone, righting the ship with her lovely daughter in tow. She seemed to be doing fine, but she asked me this question with such intensity that it threw me off kilter.

I stood on the concrete pavement, staring into space, confused, trying to understand her question, not sure I even knew what happiness was. Cars sauntered past as I digested the implications. I thought I had been happy when my children were young and we were a complete family, but that time was past and overshadowed by all that had happened since. I was hurting, exhausted, frequently triggered, and overwhelmed. I felt about as far away from happiness as I possibly could. Sidewalk, street, shapes, sky all grew distant as I pondered her point.

"I don't think that's the word I would use to describe my state of being," I said, shaking myself out of my reverie and bringing my gaze back squarely to her. "Where I am feels right, but I don't think I can say I'm happy." This answer seemed to satisfy her, and she walked away before I could return the favor. The next year I ran into this woman again and she asked me the same question. My answer was the same.

I always remembered our exchange because of her deep drive to discover my core disposition, and also because I could scarcely get my mind around the concept of happiness at that time. The angst that consumed me seemed as right as it seemed wrong. It seemed like I was where I was supposed to be, even if I didn't want to be there, and doing what I was supposed to be doing, even if I didn't want to do it. In retrospect, I think the body navigates toward health, and my body was straining to find that elusive equilibrium, even at the cost of extreme and unremitting pain.

At that point in my life, I could not even consider happiness in the midst of decompensation and reconstruction. I had to focus on calming the inner chaos and healing the inner pain. First things first. Being crazy was no environment for the attainment of happiness. The best I could hope for was staying alive.

From craziness to sanity was not an overnight affair. My craziness was transformed gradually through therapy and hard knocks. Over time, inner space for something more emerged. In the transition, I found room to breathe, and in my breath, I made space to hope, and in my hope, I had time to plan, and as I planned, I felt the urge to grow, and in my growth, I moved toward sanity, and in my sanity, I found happiness. Happiness, I found, was the result of sanity.

Today, if the beautiful mother of a former student came to me and asked, "Lyn, are you happy?" I would look into her azure-blue eyes and say, "Yes."

ACKNOWLEDGMENTS

The people I wish to thank most in this book are the ones who may never read it. They are my four (yes, four) children whose names, genders, and ages have been changed to protect their privacy. The details of their lives remain but are attached to the fictional characters in the memoir. Our collective walk back from each of our own abysses was hard work. I never tried to impose my story onto them, and I believe the decision to read this memoir has to be theirs and theirs alone.

I thank my children for loving me in spite of my many flaws as a parent. I thank them for forgiving me for abandoning them emotionally when I had to save myself. I thank them for remembering their childhoods as less traumatic than I remember them. I thank them for growing up and becoming the people they are supposed to be. I thank them for letting me love them—with all my heart—in my own imperfect way.

The next person I wish to thank is Sonia. I often felt as if she were my mother. She mothered me—in the best sense of that word—in a way that allowed me to grow up even though I was already forty-four years old when I started working with her. Although she always kept professional boundaries, I knew she loved me. Isn't that where healing happens? In a setting that allows for someone to love you? Under her care, I was able to reconstruct what had been deconstructed. I walked the journey from craziness to sanity. I was reborn. I reclaimed my life from the shadow of traumatic memory.

I am deeply indebted to those who were willing to read my manuscript in different stages of development and give me unvarnished critique: Sonia Nowak, Rev. Tilda Norberg, Rev. Dr. Bruce Epperly, Gail Coleman, Rhoda Glick, Rev. Cheryl Stoneback, Dr. Michael Crabtree, and Linda Crockett; and to Rev. Dan. Moser, Ann Sheridan, and Paul McAndrew for reading targeted portions for accuracy. A special thanks to Gail Coleman, who was my greatest cheerleader and read multiple versions of the manuscript, and to Linda Crockett, who wrote the foreword and invited me to be interviewed by Safe Communities in Lancaster, Pennsylvania. Thank you to Moravian College, especially Lisa Brand, director of development, who helped me reconstruct the beauty of the Moravian Christmas Vespers, and Central Moravian Church.

My memoir would have looked very different without the sage guidance of my editor Sarah Chauncey, who believed I had a story to tell and held my feet to the fire until it came out right. Thank you, Sarah! Many thanks to John Koehler and the whole staff at Koehler Books, who walked with me every step of the way toward publication. I can't forget the women and men in the Dissociative Writers Workshops who continue to inspire me with the power and raw authenticity of their words. Together, we are learning to open our hearts, trust, and support one another on the writing path.

From 2001 to 2021, the Prayer House Community became my chosen family after I was integrated and creating a life with intimate relationships. Special thanks to Tilda, George, Peter, Anna, Rhoda, Janet, Deborah, and Kim. With their loving kindness and compassion, I was able to put to work all the lessons I had learned about intimacy in the previous ten years of therapy. Were it not for them, I doubt I would be happily married today.

Finally, I wish to thank my second and third husbands, the late

Ronald Greene Barrett and Ronald Wayne Bussian. Ron Greene lived only a year after we married, but his love and our relationship showed me that I could, indeed, function well in a loving relationship. Ron Wayne has been the companion and lover I have always longed for. He is smart, gentle, and trustworthy, and he has been patient with both himself and me as we have navigated together the inevitable triggers an intimate relationship sets off. He has been nothing but encouraging in the writing of this memoir. Once again, love wins.

Praise and thanks to God for life, love, and every breath of every moment of every day. Thank you even for the shadows, out of which I reclaimed my life. It's all gift.

IF YOU NEED HELP . . .

If you think you may have been abused and/or have dissociative symptoms, seek a therapist who has experience with dissociative clients or who is willing to learn. Remember, you are employing the therapist, so take the time to learn about them, see if they're a good fit, and use your best judgement. A good rule of thumb for evaluating a therapist's ability to work with DID clients is whether they are willing to welcome and work with your parts individually and your system as a whole.

For a therapist referral, ask your family physician or another professional person you know and trust, ask family or friends for a referral, or search the internet for referrals. The Sidran Institute: Traumatic Stress Education and Advocacy offers a Help Desk that locates therapists with appropriate training in dissociative disorders in regions throughout the United States at 410-825-8888, Ext. 102. Other resources may be found at the International Society for the Study of Trauma and Dissociation (ISSTD) at 844-994-7783.

The National Suicide Prevention Lifeline is 1-800-273-8255 (for Spanish speakers 1-800-628-9454). They provide a 24/7, toll-free hotline available to anyone in suicidal crisis or emotional distress. Call them and speak to a counselor now.

READING GROUP
DISCUSSION QUESTIONS

1. Compare and contrast Barrett's life before she learned of her husband's affair and after her "bubble burst." What signs of her future do you think Barrett missed when her life was happy as a wife and mother?

2. Barrett describes her decompensation as if she were going "crazy." Is that an apt word to use in her circumstances? What are the pros and cons of using the word crazy to describe her experiences?

3. When Barrett made an unsuccessful suicide attempt, a part of her said, "You can't even commit suicide well. You failed at that too. You're pathetic. What a wimp." Which alter do you think was speaking and why?

4. When Barrett admitted herself to a women's unit in a psychiatric hospital, she was a teacher and the head of a private school. Many of the other women in the unit were under educated, from a lower socio-economic bracket, and from homes of addiction and abuse. Yet Barrett was relieved to be in their company and said, "I'm going to fit in just fine." What do you think she meant by that?

5. Barrett identified her love for her children as central to her identity, but she lost that love when an alter fled for safety. Although she made efforts to reestablish her relationships with her children, were there other ways, within the confines of her disorder, that she could have repaired the breach?

6. Were Barrett's depictions of her fifteen alters helpful in understanding her story? Discuss the ways her different alters functioned in her system.

7. Barrett defined the terms dissociation, depersonalization, derealization, decompensation, transference, projection, and gaslighting to describe her experiences. Was it helpful to have this information included in the memoir? Did she give you enough information or did it make you want to learn more about these terms?

8. How did Barrett's faith journey interact with her desire to heal? Do you think it was concurrent with but extraneous to her healing, or central to it?

9. Barrett wanted explicit, front-brain memories to explain away her "craziness." She healed her symptoms and integrated her personalities in spite of the fact that concrete memories were not available. Based on how the book described traumatic memory, how would you explain that?

10. Some people with dissociative identity disorder heal their symptoms but choose to remain in healthy parts as "functional multiples." Barrett's alters chose, instead, to integrate into one whole. What are the advantages and disadvantages of each choice?

11. Although current research into traumatic memory and dissociative identity disorder confirms that between 1 and 5 % of the world population has the disorder in response to chronic childhood trauma, it is still a controversial diagnosis in some circles. Why do you think that is so?

12. Did you come away with a better understanding of dissociative identity disorder? What questions did Barrett's memoir leave you with?

Everything
everybody
feels is

okay, valid
and
important.